ULTIMATE
ARMOUR WARS

WARREN ELLIS • STEVE KURTH

ARMOUR WARS

Writer
Warren Ellis

Artist
Steve Kurth

Colorist
Guru EFX

Letterer
VC's Joe Sabino

Cover Art
Brandon Peterson

Assistant Editor
Sana Amanat

Associate Editor
Lauren Sankovitch

Senior Editor
Mark Paniccia

Editor in Chief
Joe Quesada

Publisher
Dan Buckley

MARVEL®

presents **ULTIMATE COMICS ARMOUR WARS**

ULTIMATE COMICS ARMOUR WARS. Contains material originally published in magazine form as ULTIMATE COMICS ARMOUR WARS #1-4. First printing 2010. Published by Panini Publishing, a division of Panini UK Limited. Mike Riddell, Managing Director. Alan O'Keefe, Managing Editor. Mark Irvine, Production Manager. Marco M. Lupoi, Publishing Director Europe. Ed Hammond, Reprint Editor. Alex Foot and William Lucas, Designers. Office of publication: Brockbourne House, 77 Mount Ephraim, Tunbridge Wells, Kent TN4 8BS. MARVEL, IRON MAN and all related characters: TM & © 2010 Marvel Entertainment, LLC and its subsidiaries. Licensed by Marvel Characters B.V. www.marvel.com. All rights reserved. No similarity between any of the names, characters, persons and/or institutions in this edition with those of any living or dead person or institution is intended, and any such similarity which may exist is purely coincidental. This publication may not be sold, except by authorised dealers, and is sold subject to the condition that it shall not be sold or distributed with any part of its cover or markings removed, nor in a mutilated condition. Licensed by Marvel Characters B.V. www.marvel.com. All rights reserved. Printed in Italy. ISBN: 978-1-84653-441-6

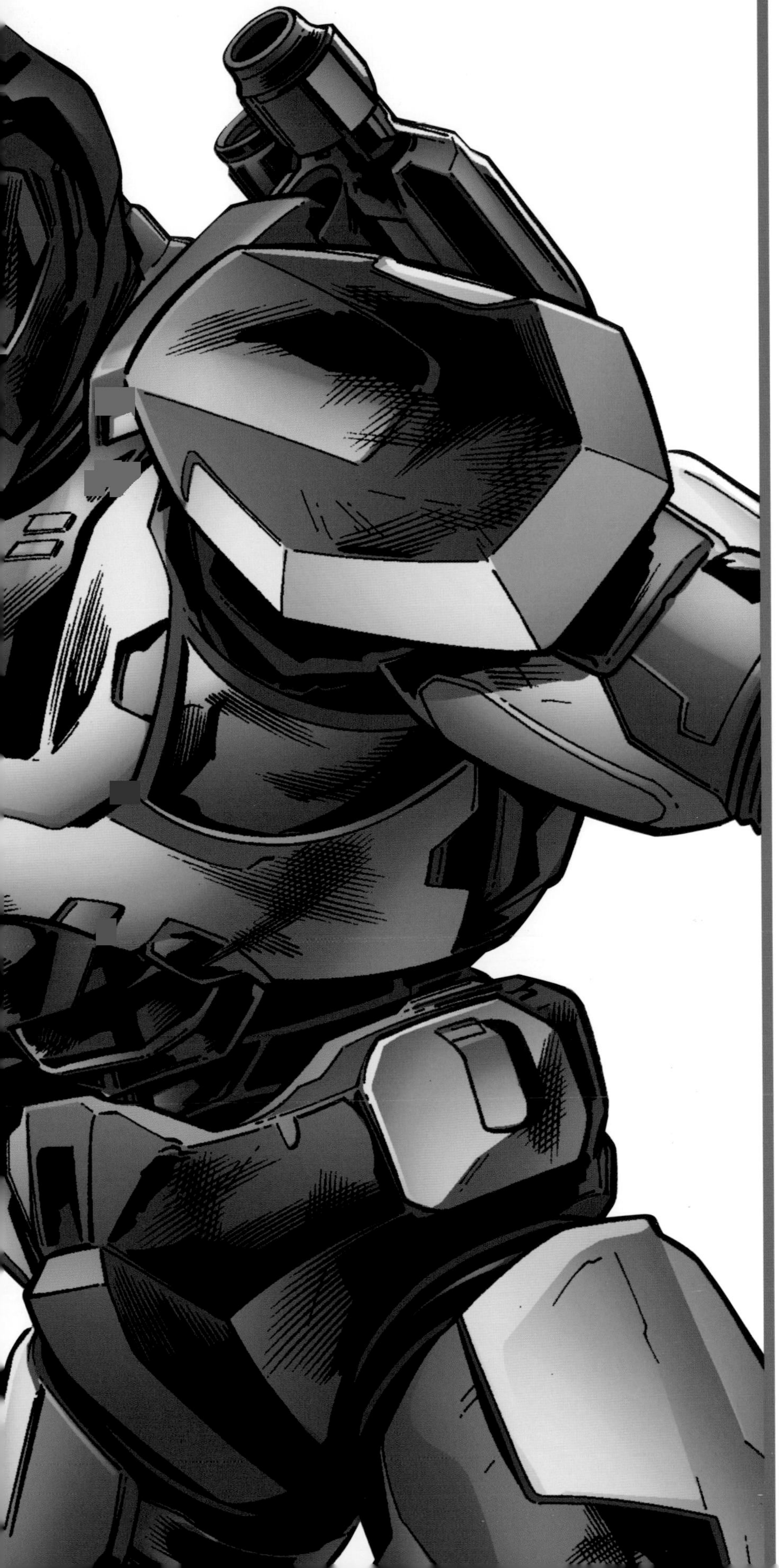

ARMOUR WARS

ULTIMATE
ARMOUR WARS™

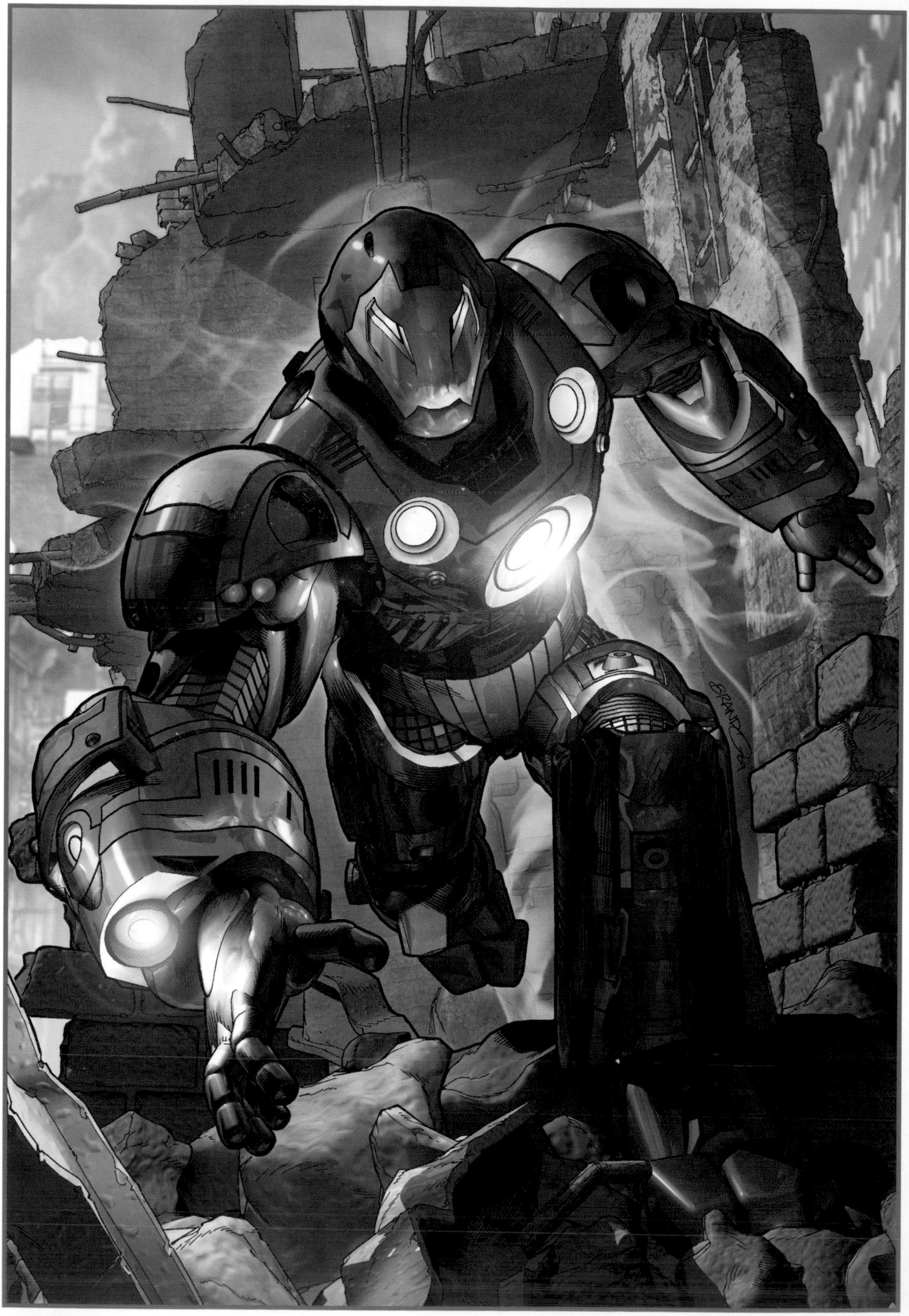

MARVEL®

ISSUE 001 COVER

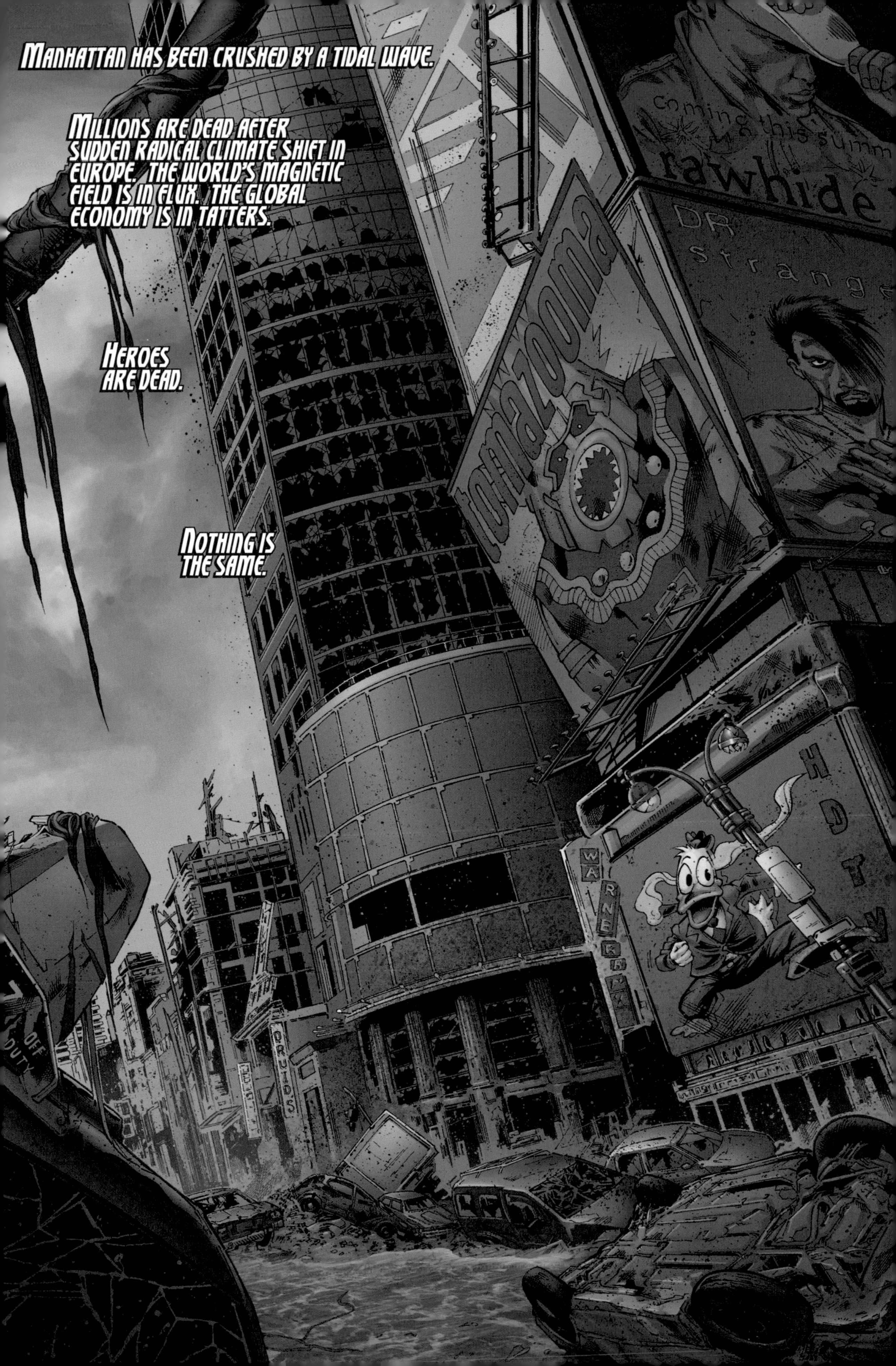
MANHATTAN HAS BEEN CRUSHED BY A TIDAL WAVE.
MILLIONS ARE DEAD AFTER SUDDEN RADICAL CLIMATE SHIFT IN EUROPE. THE WORLD'S MAGNETIC FIELD IS IN FLUX. THE GLOBAL ECONOMY IS IN TATTERS.
HEROES ARE DEAD.
NOTHING IS THE SAME.
rawhide
DR strange
tomazooma
HDTV
DRUID'S
OFF DUTY

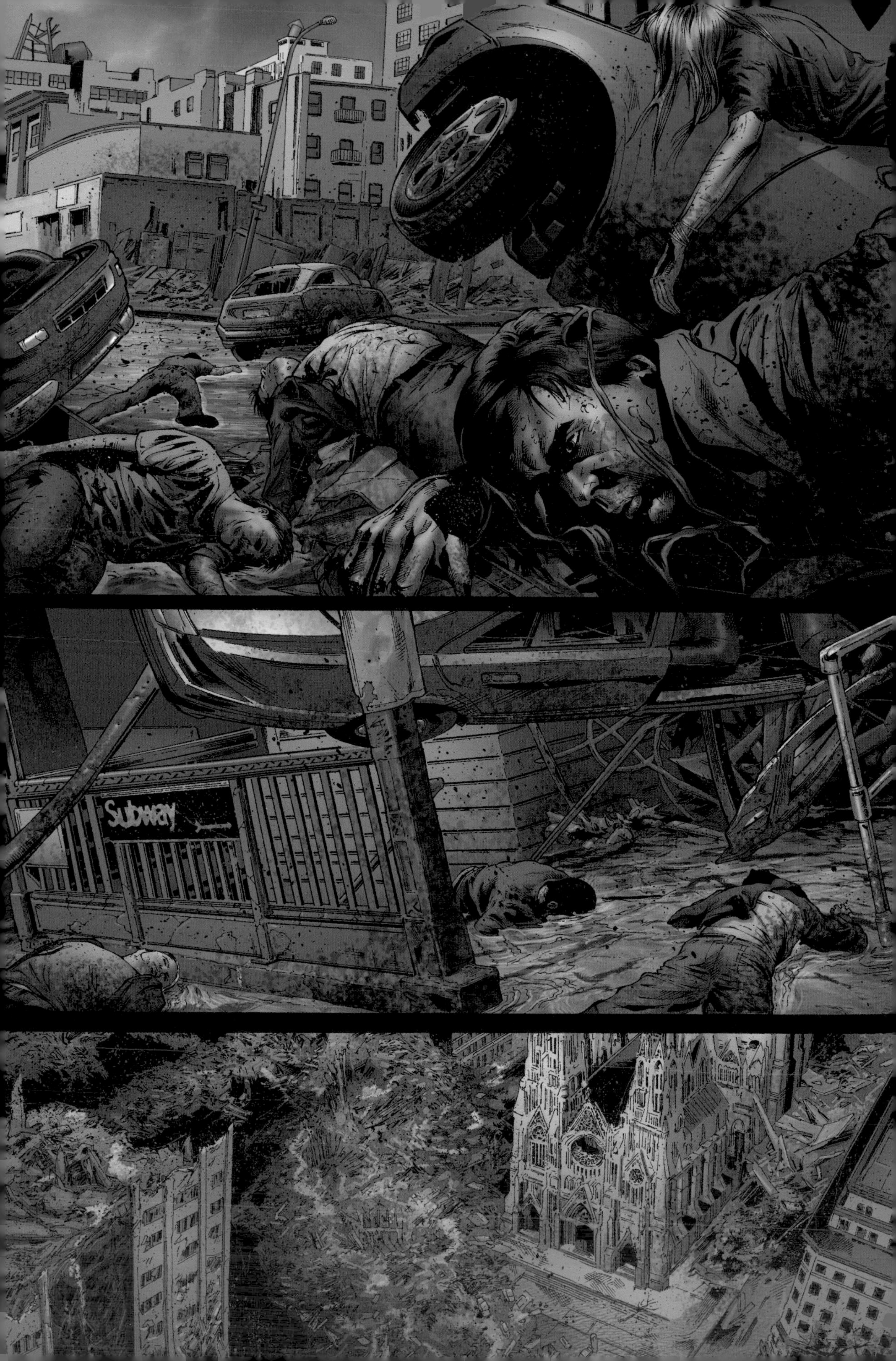
Subway

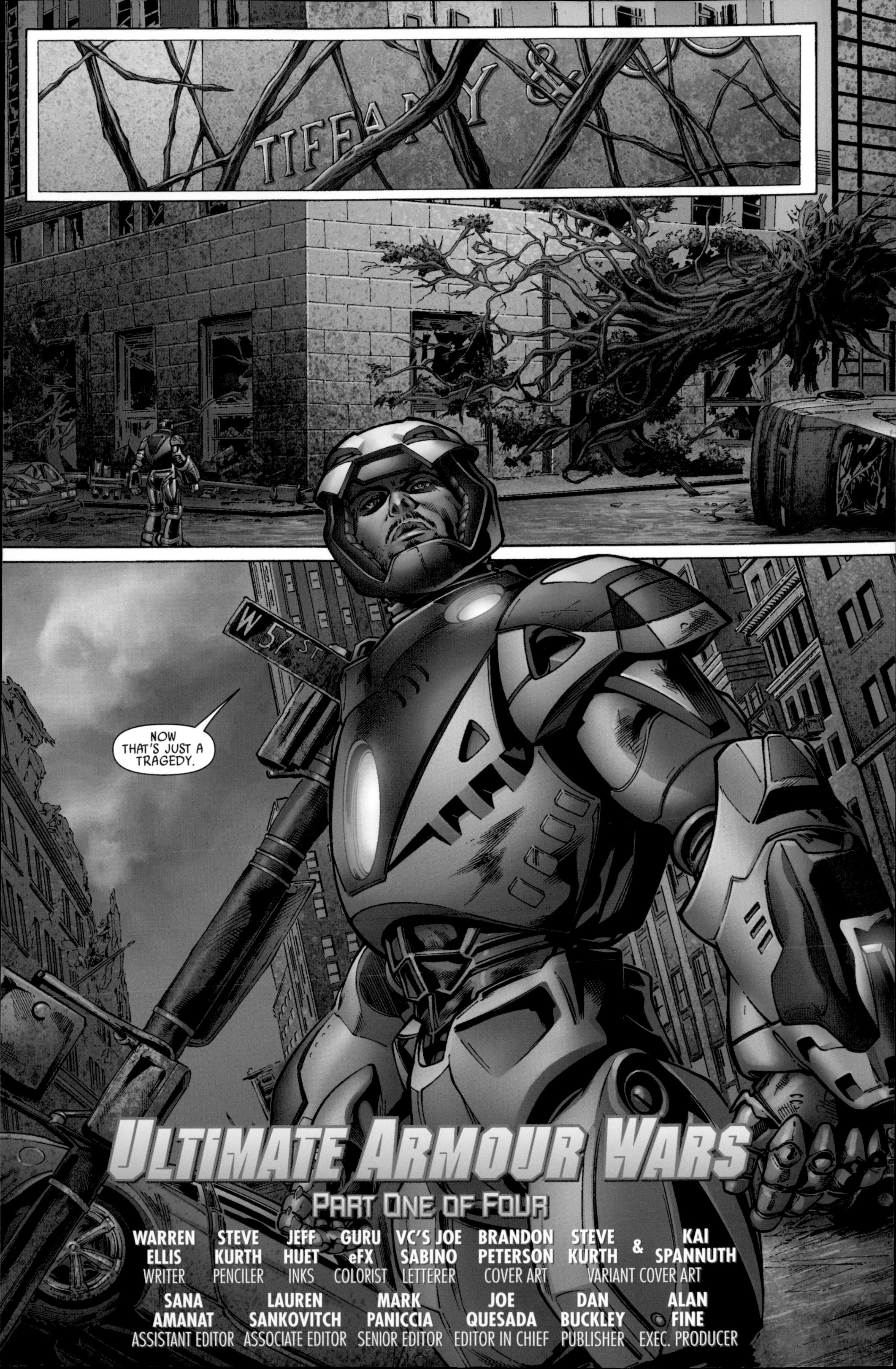
W 57 ST
NOW THAT'S JUST A TRAGEDY.
ULTIMATE ARMOUR WARS
PART ONE OF FOUR
WARREN ELLIS WRITER
STEVE KURTH PENCILER
JEFF HUET INKS
GURU eFX COLORIST
VC'S JOE SABINO LETTERER
BRANDON PETERSON COVER ART
STEVE KURTH & KAI SPANNUTH VARIANT COVER ART
SANA AMANAT ASSISTANT EDITOR
LAUREN SANKOVITCH ASSOCIATE EDITOR
MARK PANICCIA SENIOR EDITOR
JOE QUESADA EDITOR IN CHIEF
DAN BUCKLEY PUBLISHER
ALAN FINE EXEC. PRODUCER

TONY? WE'RE GETTING A WEIRD GHOSTING EFFECT ON YOUR RADAR.

CAN'T PIN IT DOWN, AND YOUR ONBOARD MOTION SENSORS KEEP CUTTING OUT, TOO. YOU SEEING ANYTHING?

PLENTY OF GHOSTS.

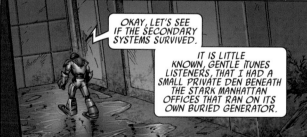

OKAY, LET'S SEE IF THE SECONDARY SYSTEMS SURVIVED.

IT IS LITTLE KNOWN, GENTLE ITUNES LISTENERS, THAT I HAD A SMALL PRIVATE DEN BENEATH THE STARK MANHATTAN OFFICES THAT RAN ON ITS OWN BURIED GENERATOR.

OH, HOW ABOUT THAT... WHO WOULD BELIEVE THAT SO MANY PEOPLE TOLD ME PLACING AN EXPERIMENTAL REACTOR UNDER MANHATTAN WAS A SILLY AND POTENTIALLY LETHAL IDEA?

I'M A @$#%$#% GENIUS.

WOULDN'T WANT US TO GET AN ADULT RATING FOR SPEAKING LIKE REAL PEOPLE OR ANYTHING.

BETTER EDIT THAT LAST BIT, HAPPY.

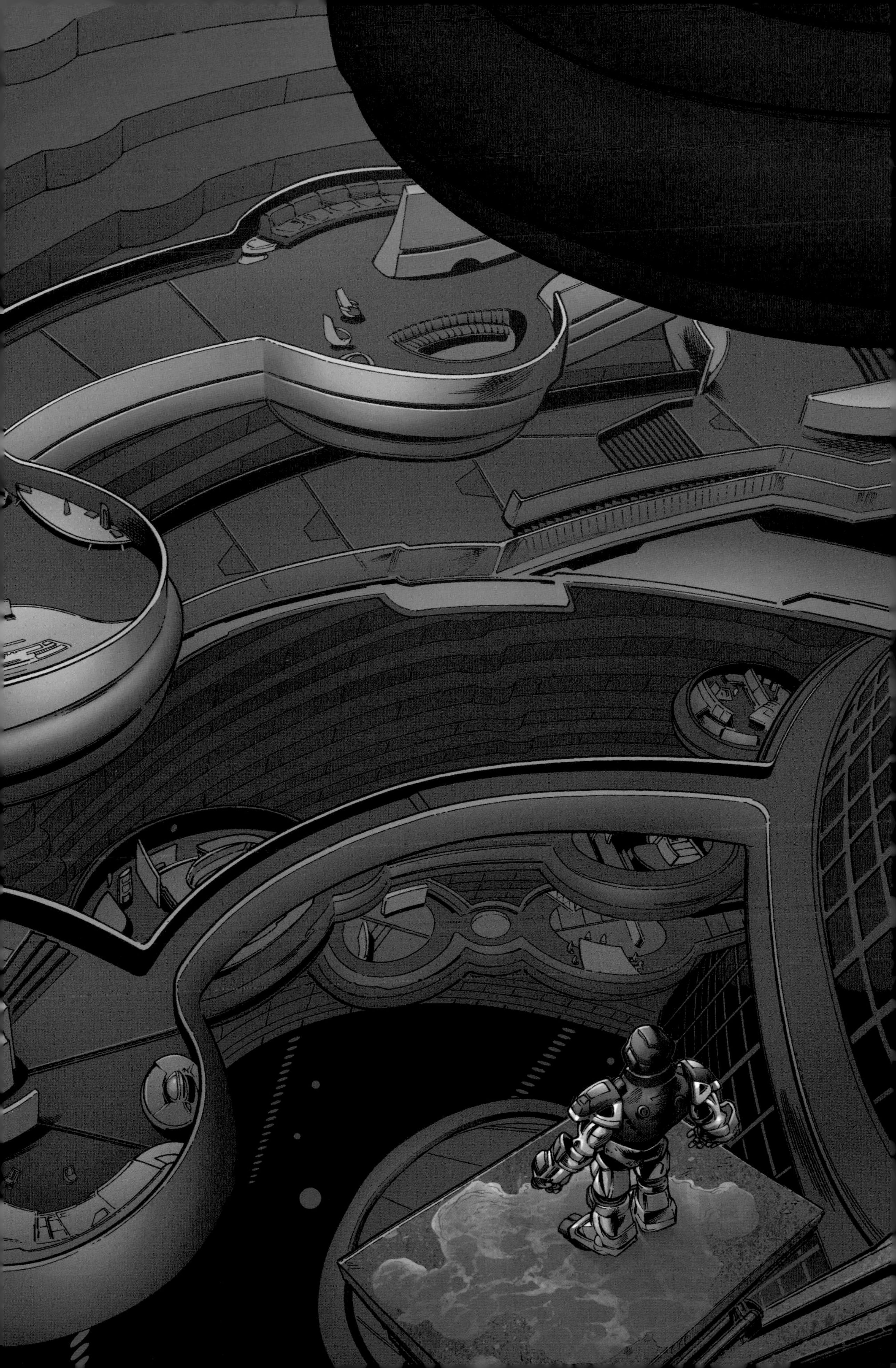

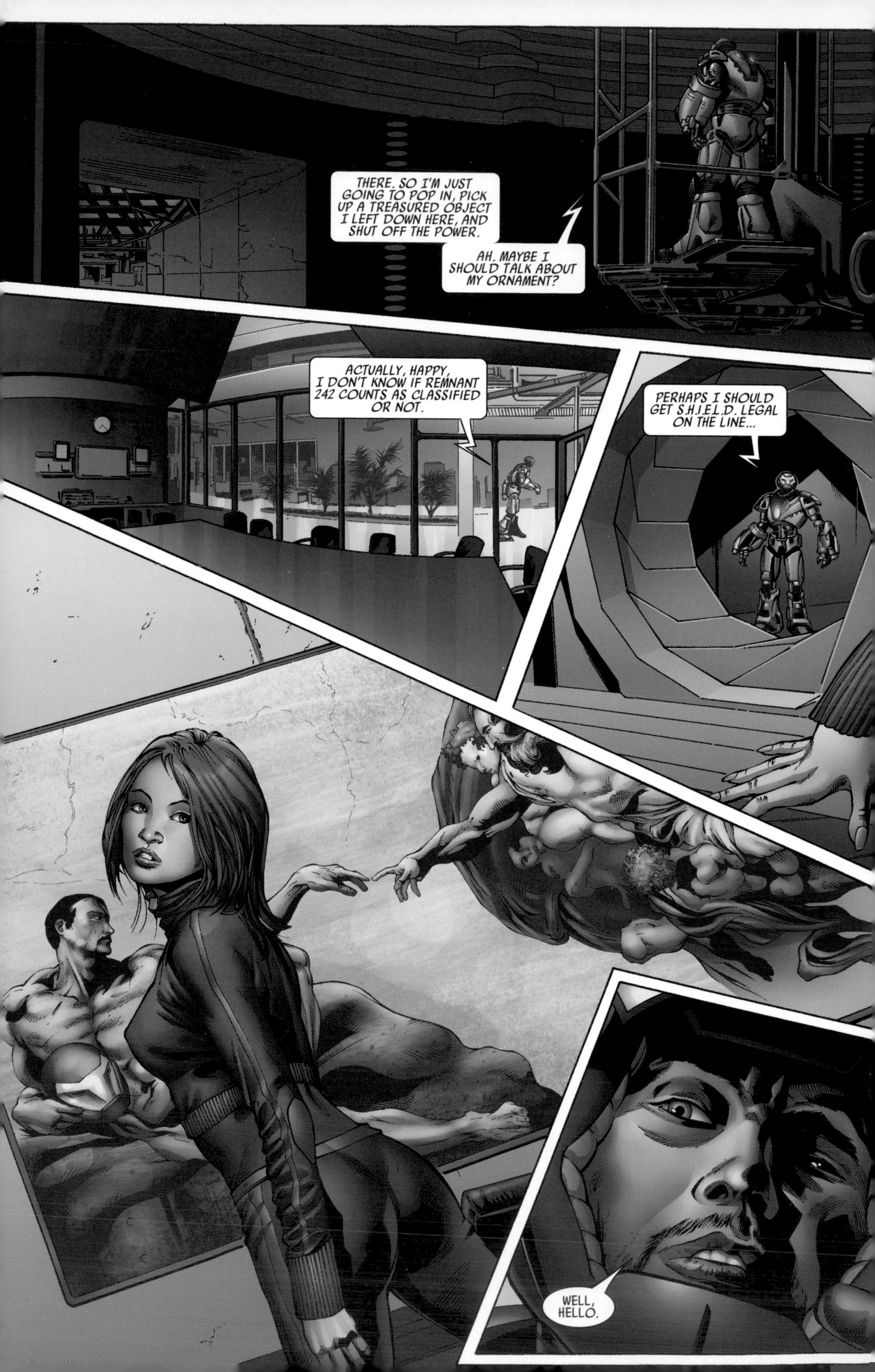
THERE. SO I'M JUST GOING TO POP IN, PICK UP A TREASURED OBJECT I LEFT DOWN HERE, AND SHUT OFF THE POWER.
AH. MAYBE I SHOULD TALK ABOUT MY ORNAMENT?
ACTUALLY, HAPPY, I DON'T KNOW IF REMNANT 242 COUNTS AS CLASSIFIED OR NOT.
PERHAPS I SHOULD GET S.H.I.E.L.D. LEGAL ON THE LINE...
WELL, HELLO.

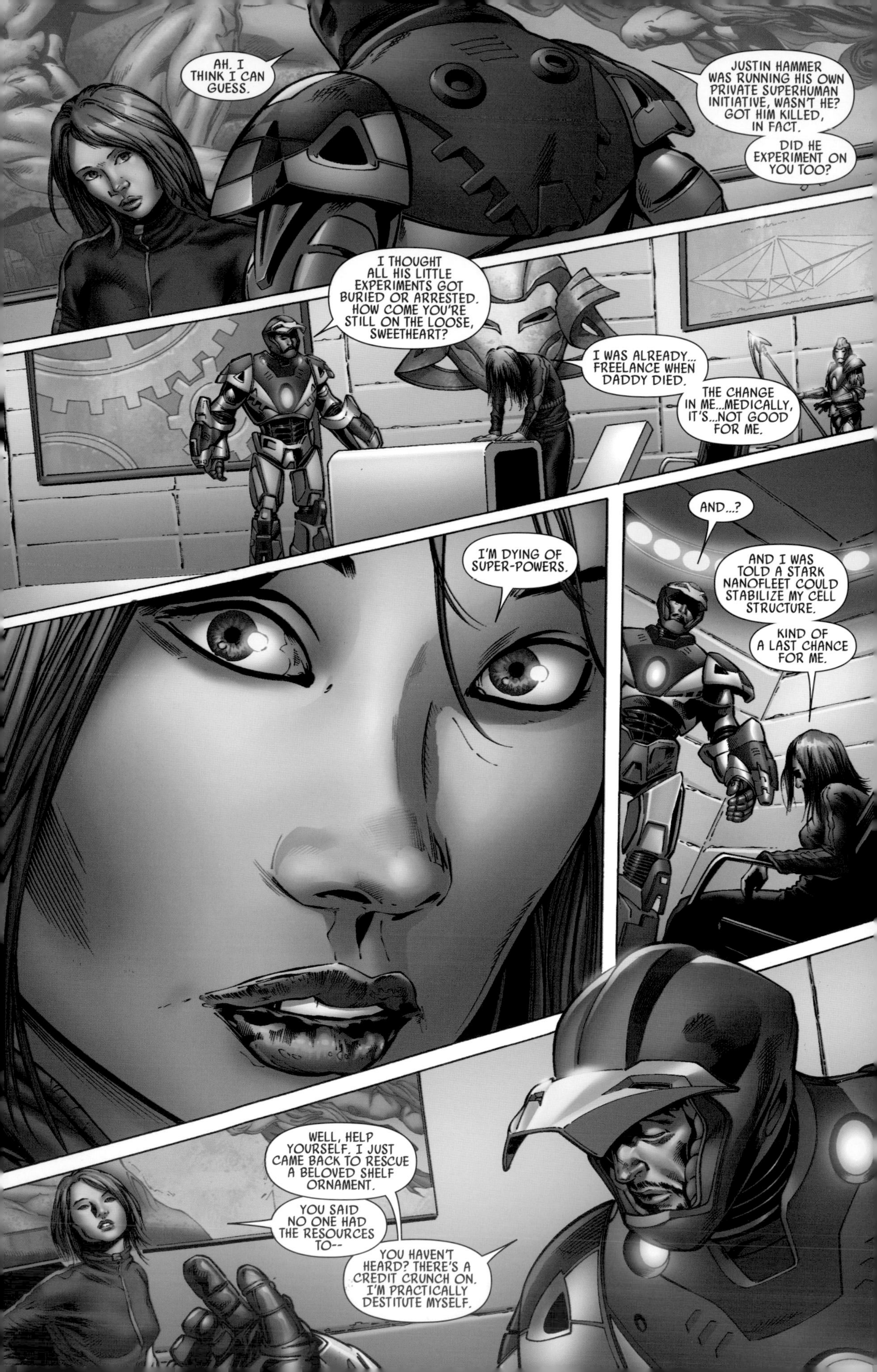

AH. I THINK I CAN GUESS.
JUSTIN HAMMER WAS RUNNING HIS OWN PRIVATE SUPERHUMAN INITIATIVE, WASN'T HE? GOT HIM KILLED, IN FACT.
DID HE EXPERIMENT ON YOU TOO?
I THOUGHT ALL HIS LITTLE EXPERIMENTS GOT BURIED OR ARRESTED. HOW COME YOU'RE STILL ON THE LOOSE, SWEETHEART?
I WAS ALREADY... FREELANCE WHEN DADDY DIED.
THE CHANGE IN ME...MEDICALLY, IT'S...NOT GOOD FOR ME.
I'M DYING OF SUPER-POWERS.
AND...?
AND I WAS TOLD A STARK NANOFLEET COULD STABILIZE MY CELL STRUCTURE.
KIND OF A LAST CHANCE FOR ME.
WELL, HELP YOURSELF. I JUST CAME BACK TO RESCUE A BELOVED SHELF ORNAMENT.
YOU SAID NO ONE HAD THE RESOURCES TO--
YOU HAVEN'T HEARD? THERE'S A CREDIT CRUNCH ON. I'M PRACTICALLY DESTITUTE MYSELF.

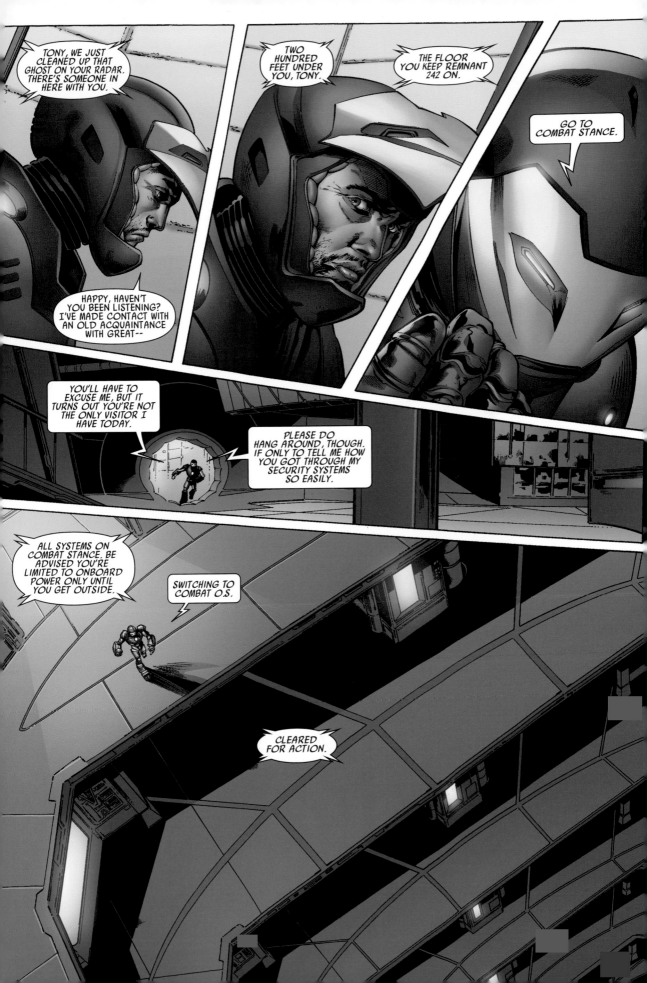

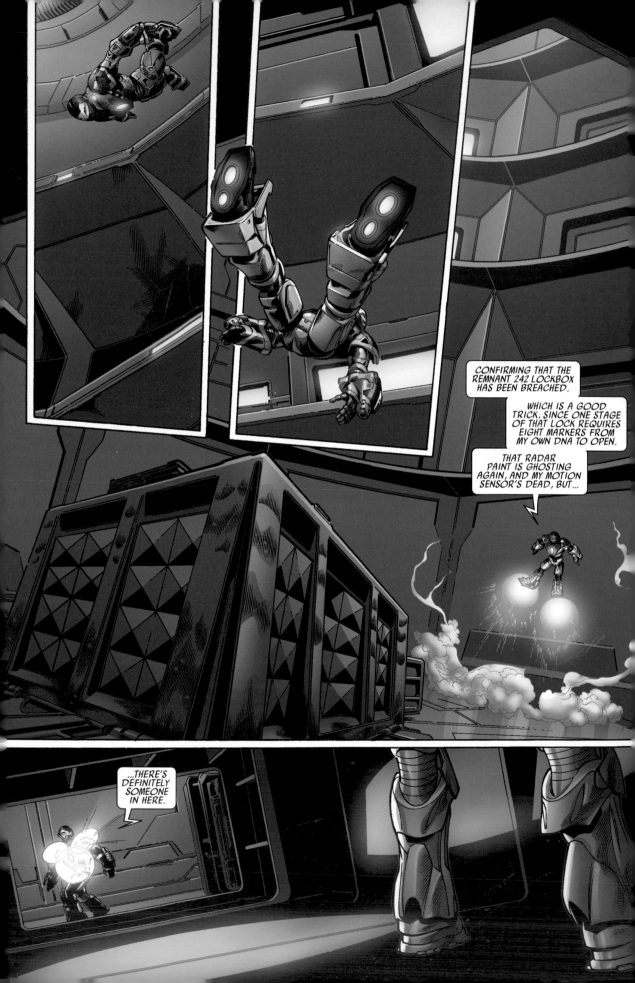

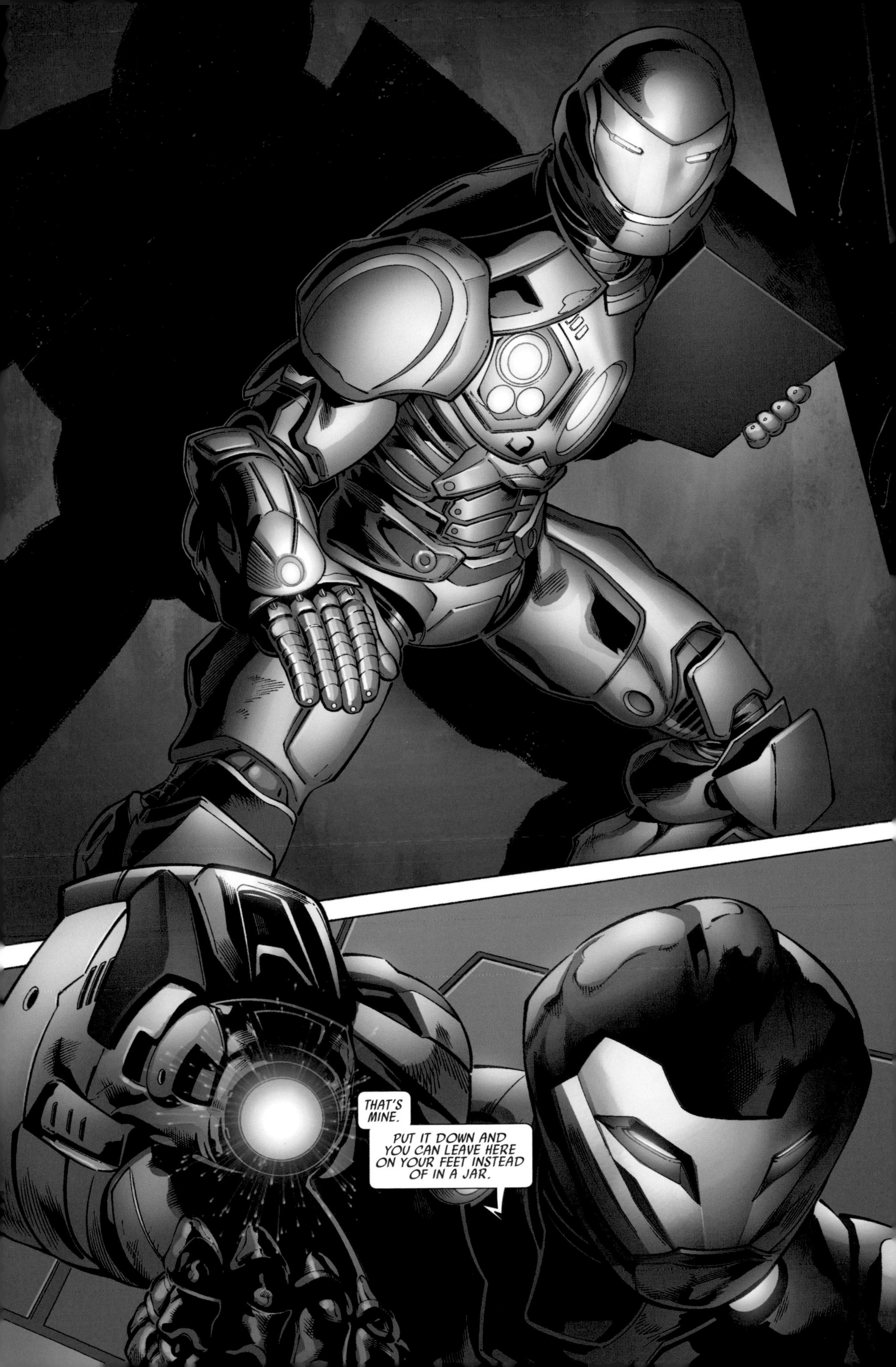
THAT'S MINE.
PUT IT DOWN AND YOU CAN LEAVE HERE ON YOUR FEET INSTEAD OF IN A JAR.

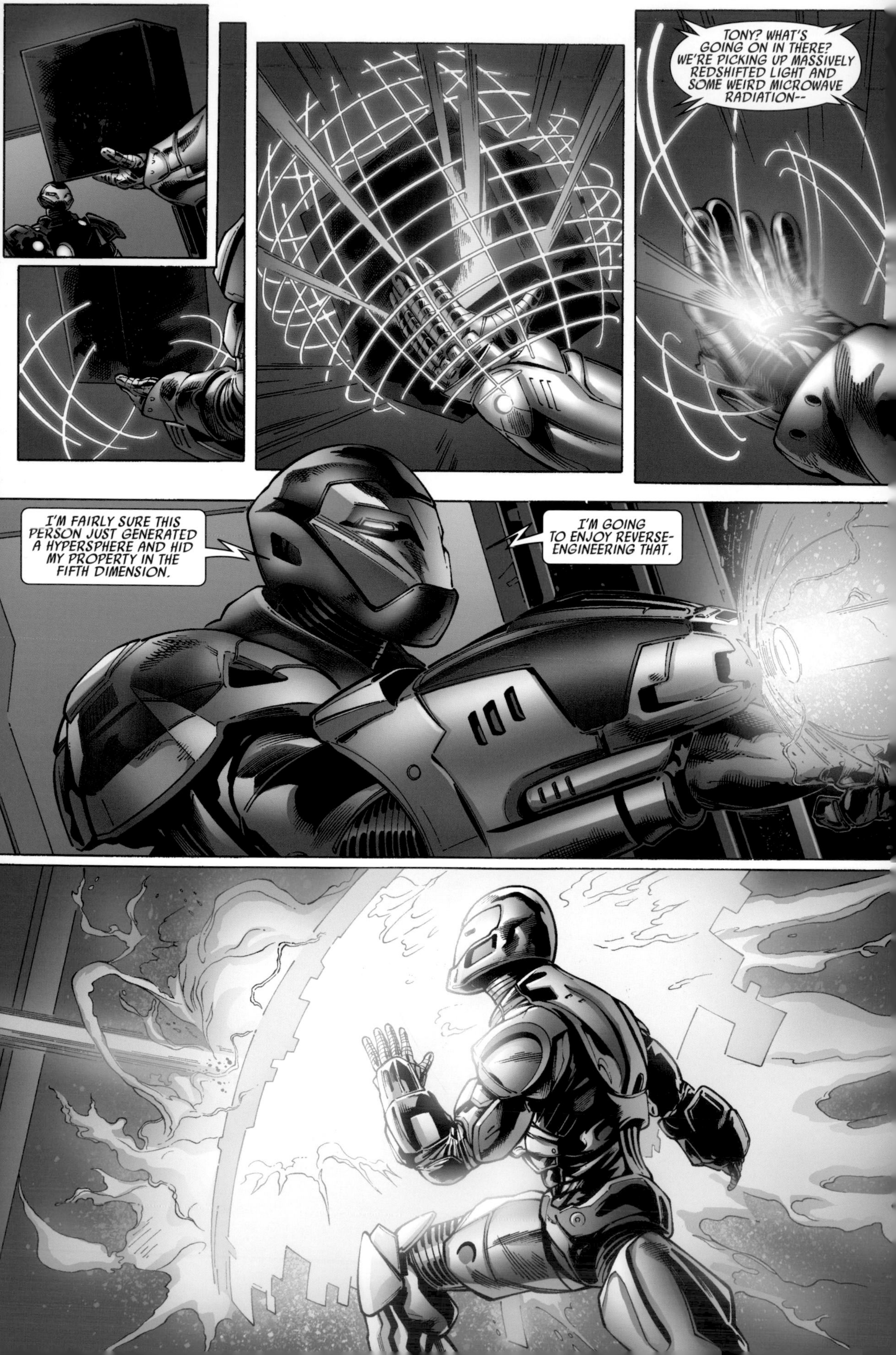
TONY? WHAT'S GOING ON IN THERE? WE'RE PICKING UP MASSIVELY REDSHIFTED LIGHT AND SOME WEIRD MICROWAVE RADIATION--
I'M FAIRLY SURE THIS PERSON JUST GENERATED A HYPERSPHERE AND HID MY PROPERTY IN THE FIFTH DIMENSION.
I'M GOING TO ENJOY REVERSE-ENGINEERING THAT.

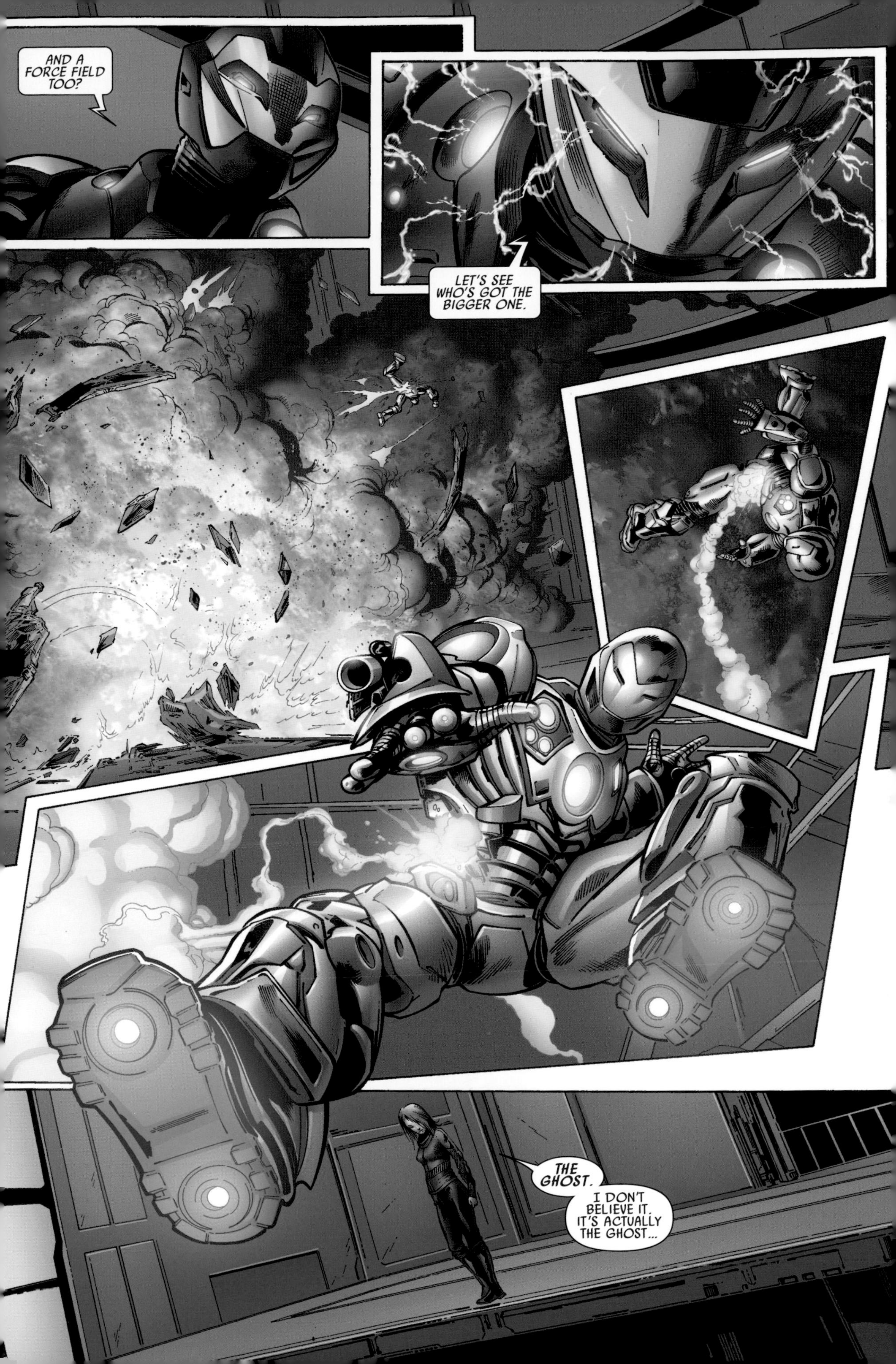
AND A FORCE FIELD TOO?
LET'S SEE WHO'S GOT THE BIGGER ONE.
THE GHOST.
I DON'T BELIEVE IT. IT'S ACTUALLY THE GHOST...

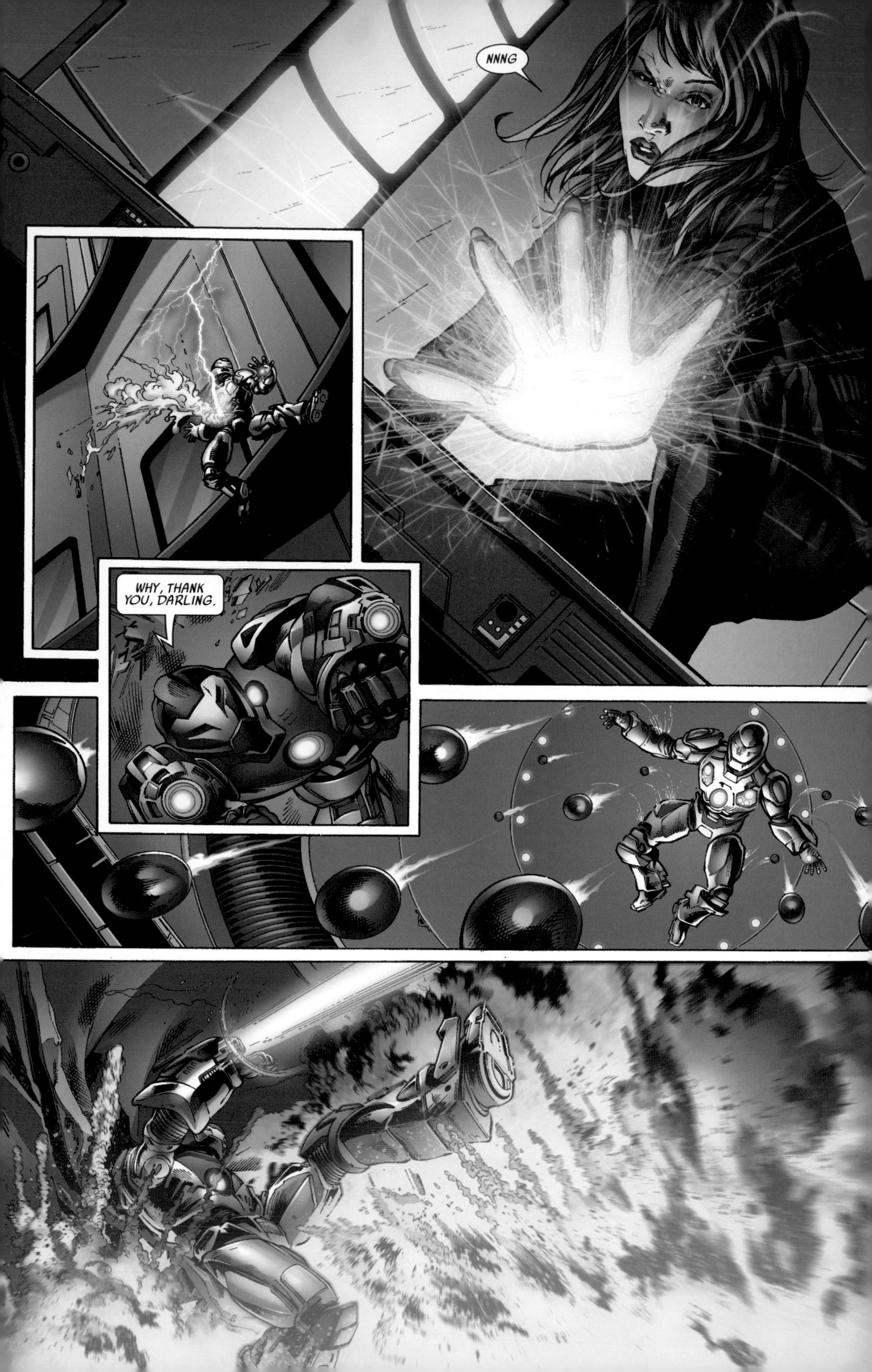
NNNG
WHY, THANK YOU, DARLING.

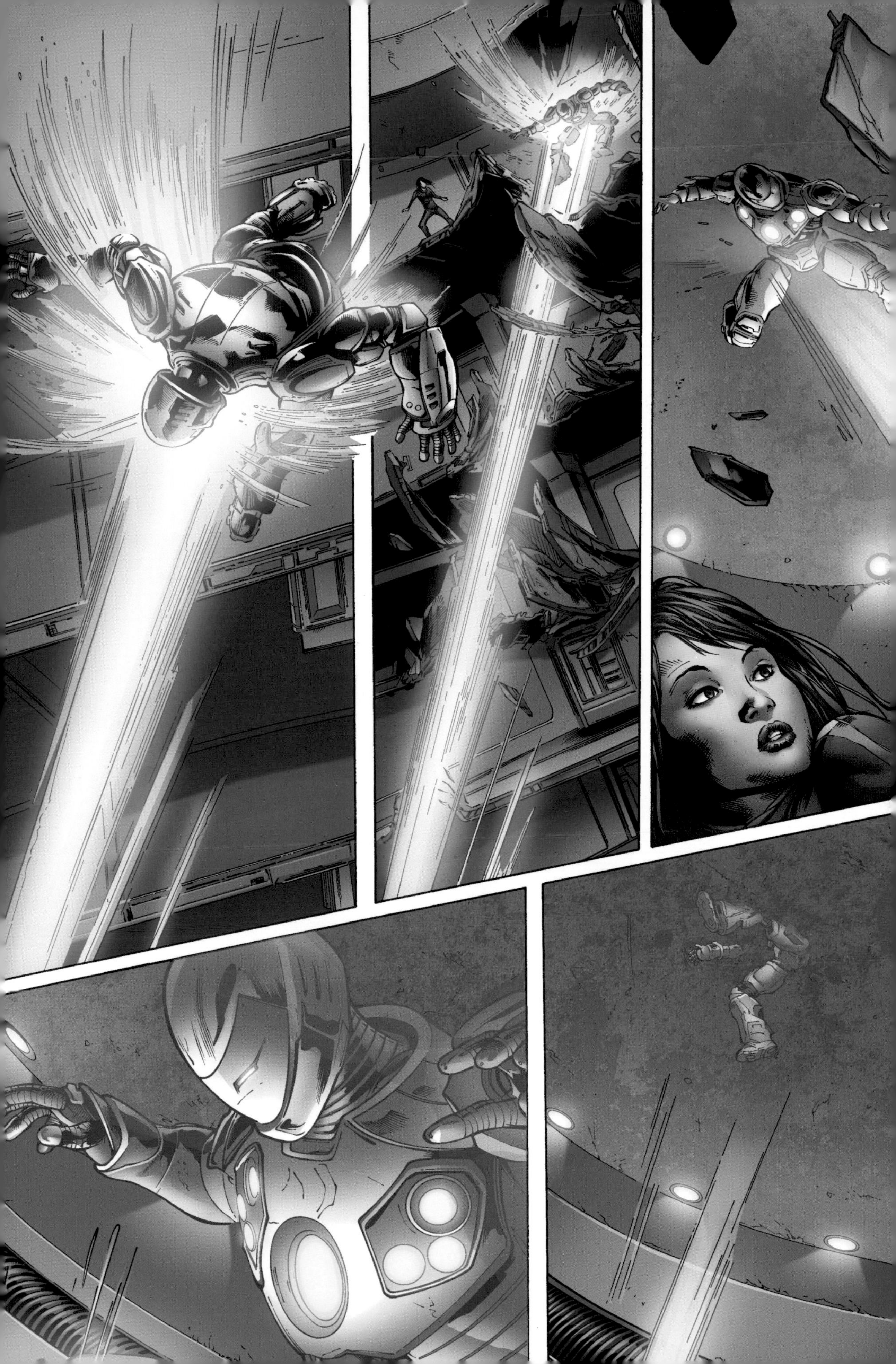

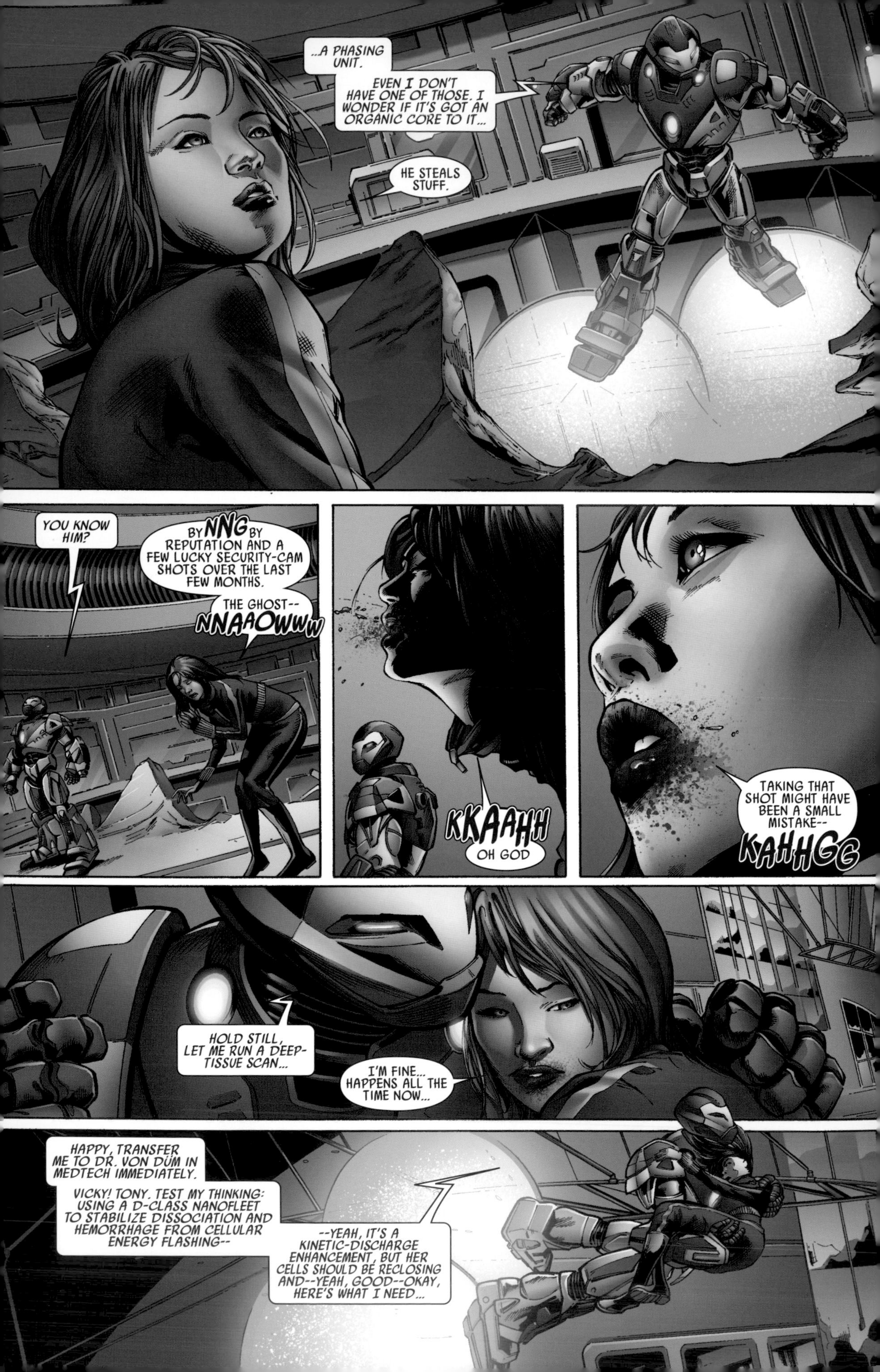
...A PHASING UNIT.
EVEN I DON'T HAVE ONE OF THOSE. I WONDER IF IT'S GOT AN ORGANIC CORE TO IT...
HE STEALS STUFF.
YOU KNOW HIM?
BY NNG BY REPUTATION AND A FEW LUCKY SECURITY-CAM SHOTS OVER THE LAST FEW MONTHS.
THE GHOST--
NNAAOWWW
KKAAHH
OH GOD
TAKING THAT SHOT MIGHT HAVE BEEN A SMALL MISTAKE--
KAHHGG
HOLD STILL, LET ME RUN A DEEP-TISSUE SCAN...
I'M FINE... HAPPENS ALL THE TIME NOW...
HAPPY, TRANSFER ME TO DR. VON DÜM IN MEDTECH IMMEDIATELY.
VICKY! TONY. TEST MY THINKING: USING A D-CLASS NANOFLEET TO STABILIZE DISSOCIATION AND HEMORRHAGE FROM CELLULAR ENERGY FLASHING--
--YEAH, IT'S A KINETIC-DISCHARGE ENHANCEMENT, BUT HER CELLS SHOULD BE RECLOSING AND--YEAH, GOOD--OKAY, HERE'S WHAT I NEED...

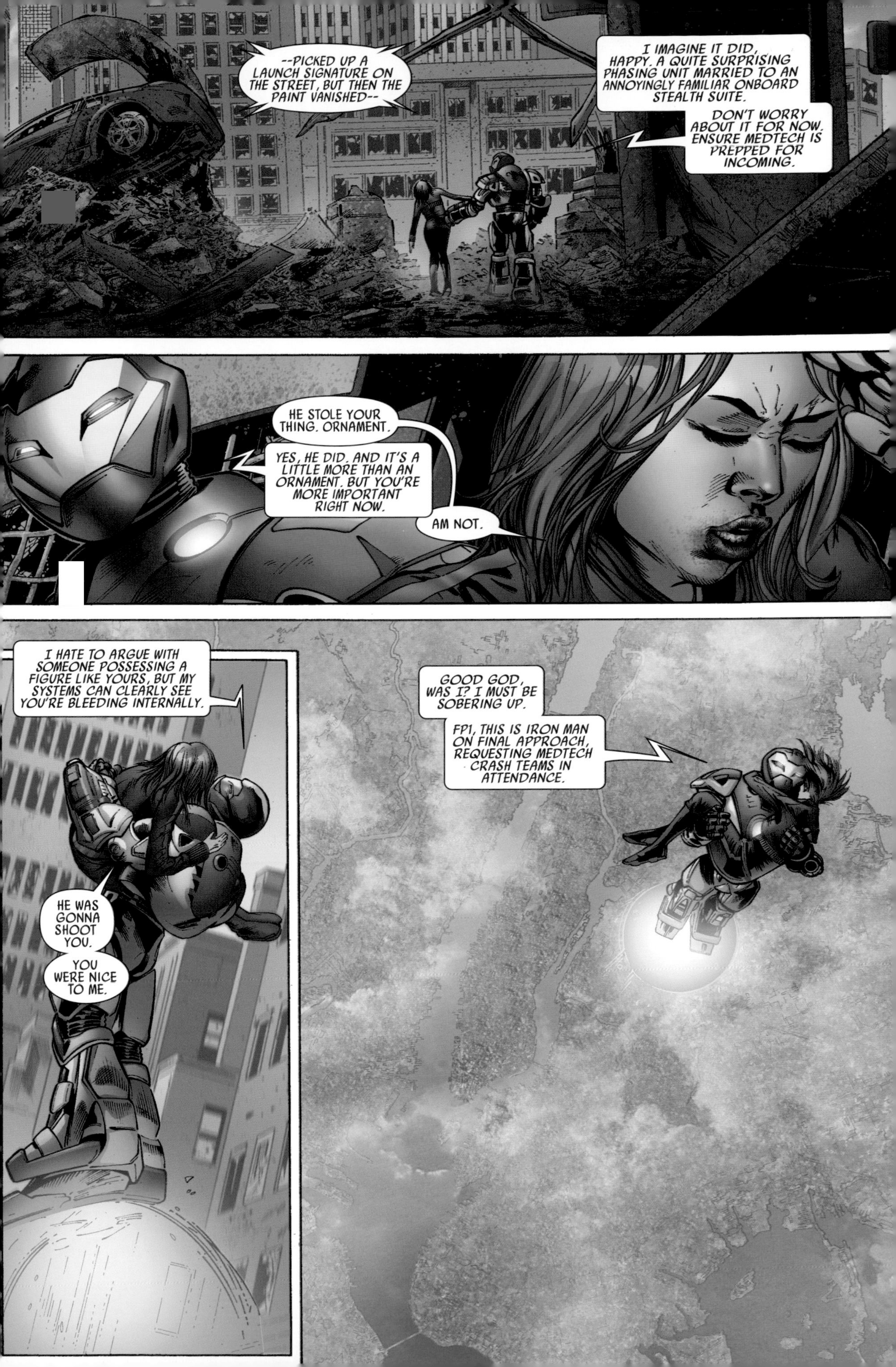
--PICKED UP A LAUNCH SIGNATURE ON THE STREET, BUT THEN THE PAINT VANISHED--
I IMAGINE IT DID, HAPPY. A QUITE SURPRISING PHASING UNIT MARRIED TO AN ANNOYINGLY FAMILIAR ONBOARD STEALTH SUITE.
DON'T WORRY ABOUT IT FOR NOW. ENSURE MEDTECH IS PREPPED FOR INCOMING.
HE STOLE YOUR THING. ORNAMENT.
YES, HE DID. AND IT'S A LITTLE MORE THAN AN ORNAMENT. BUT YOU'RE MORE IMPORTANT RIGHT NOW.
AM NOT.
I HATE TO ARGUE WITH SOMEONE POSSESSING A FIGURE LIKE YOURS, BUT MY SYSTEMS CAN CLEARLY SEE YOU'RE BLEEDING INTERNALLY.
HE WAS GONNA SHOOT YOU.
YOU WERE NICE TO ME.
GOOD GOD, WAS I? I MUST BE SOBERING UP.
FP1, THIS IS IRON MAN ON FINAL APPROACH, REQUESTING MEDTECH CRASH TEAMS IN ATTENDANCE.

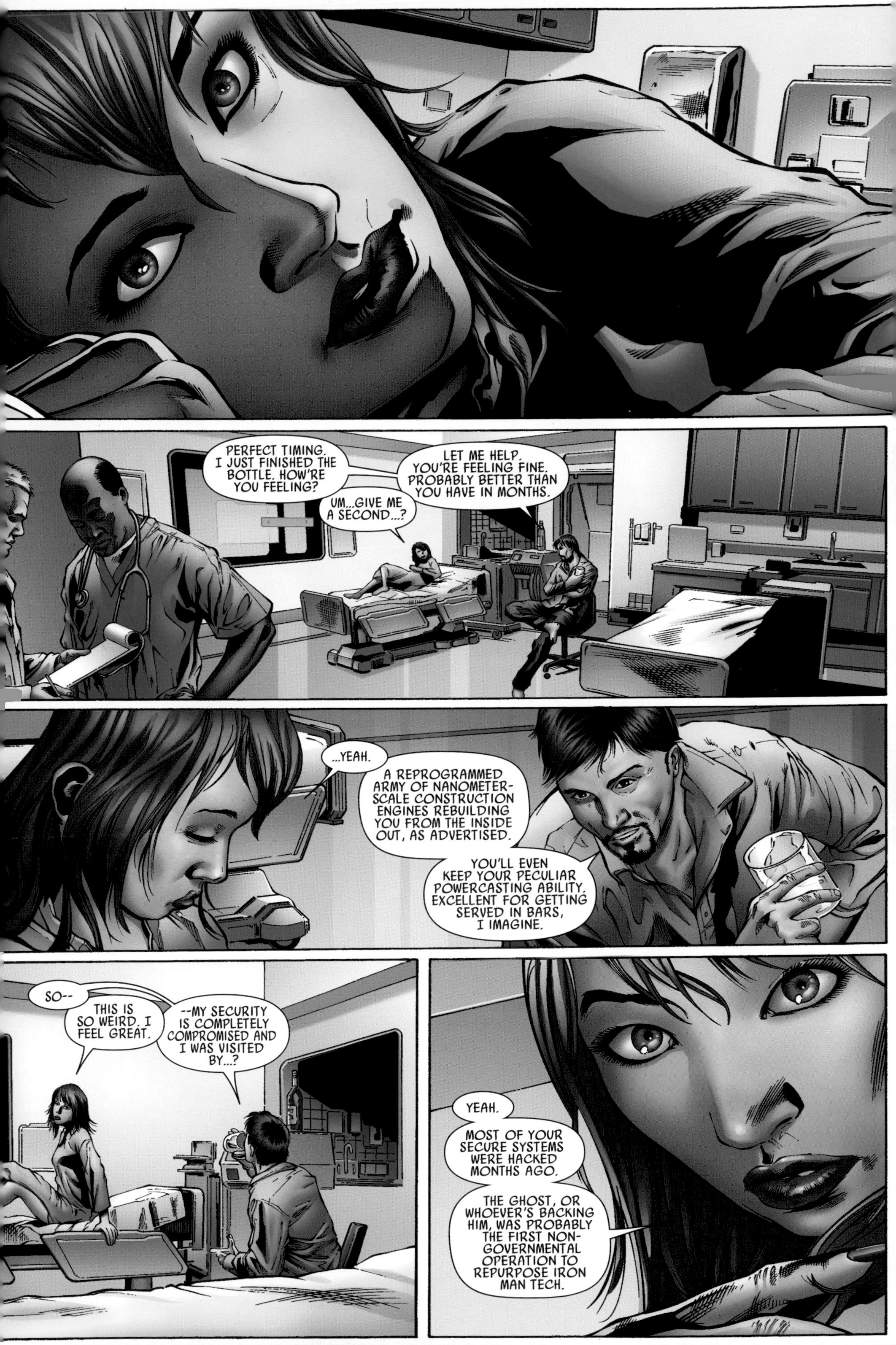

PERFECT TIMING. I JUST FINISHED THE BOTTLE. HOW'RE YOU FEELING?
UM...GIVE ME A SECOND...?
LET ME HELP. YOU'RE FEELING FINE. PROBABLY BETTER THAN YOU HAVE IN MONTHS.
...YEAH.
A REPROGRAMMED ARMY OF NANOMETER-SCALE CONSTRUCTION ENGINES REBUILDING YOU FROM THE INSIDE OUT, AS ADVERTISED.
YOU'LL EVEN KEEP YOUR PECULIAR POWERCASTING ABILITY. EXCELLENT FOR GETTING SERVED IN BARS, I IMAGINE.
SO--
THIS IS SO WEIRD. I FEEL GREAT.
--MY SECURITY IS COMPLETELY COMPROMISED AND I WAS VISITED BY...?
YEAH.
MOST OF YOUR SECURE SYSTEMS WERE HACKED MONTHS AGO.
THE GHOST, OR WHOEVER'S BACKING HIM, WAS PROBABLY THE FIRST NON-GOVERNMENTAL OPERATION TO REPURPOSE IRON MAN TECH.

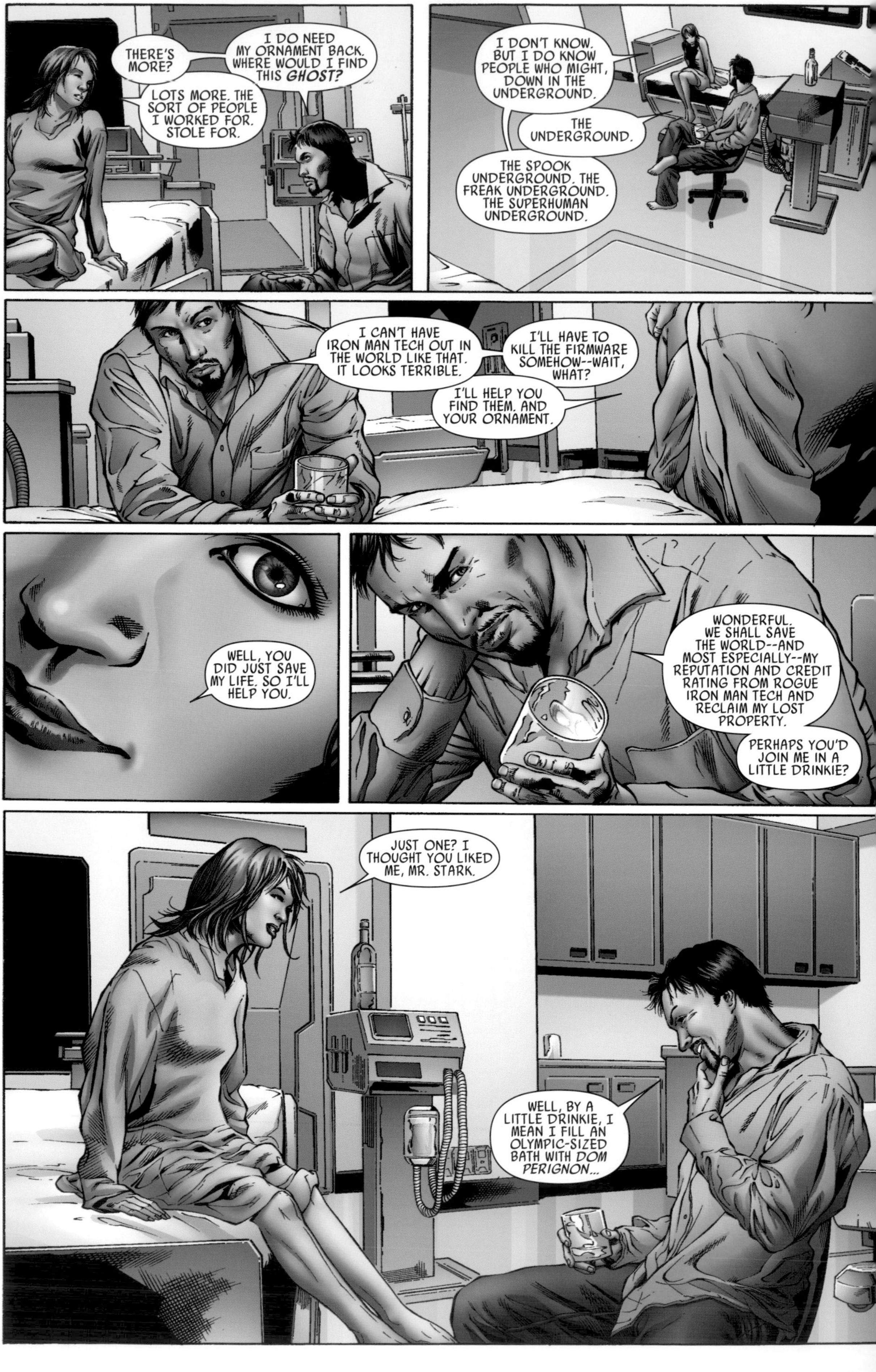
THERE'S MORE?
I DO NEED MY ORNAMENT BACK. WHERE WOULD I FIND THIS GHOST?
LOTS MORE. THE SORT OF PEOPLE I WORKED FOR. STOLE FOR.
I DON'T KNOW. BUT I DO KNOW PEOPLE WHO MIGHT, DOWN IN THE UNDERGROUND.
THE UNDERGROUND.
THE SPOOK UNDERGROUND. THE FREAK UNDERGROUND. THE SUPERHUMAN UNDERGROUND.
I CAN'T HAVE IRON MAN TECH OUT IN THE WORLD LIKE THAT. IT LOOKS TERRIBLE.
I'LL HAVE TO KILL THE FIRMWARE SOMEHOW--WAIT, WHAT?
I'LL HELP YOU FIND THEM. AND YOUR ORNAMENT.
WELL, YOU DID JUST SAVE MY LIFE. SO I'LL HELP YOU.
WONDERFUL. WE SHALL SAVE THE WORLD--AND MOST ESPECIALLY--MY REPUTATION AND CREDIT RATING FROM ROGUE IRON MAN TECH AND RECLAIM MY LOST PROPERTY.
PERHAPS YOU'D JOIN ME IN A LITTLE DRINKIE?
JUST ONE? I THOUGHT YOU LIKED ME, MR. STARK.
WELL, BY A LITTLE DRINKIE, I MEAN I FILL AN OLYMPIC-SIZED BATH WITH DOM PERIGNON...

ULTIMATE

ARMOUR WARS™

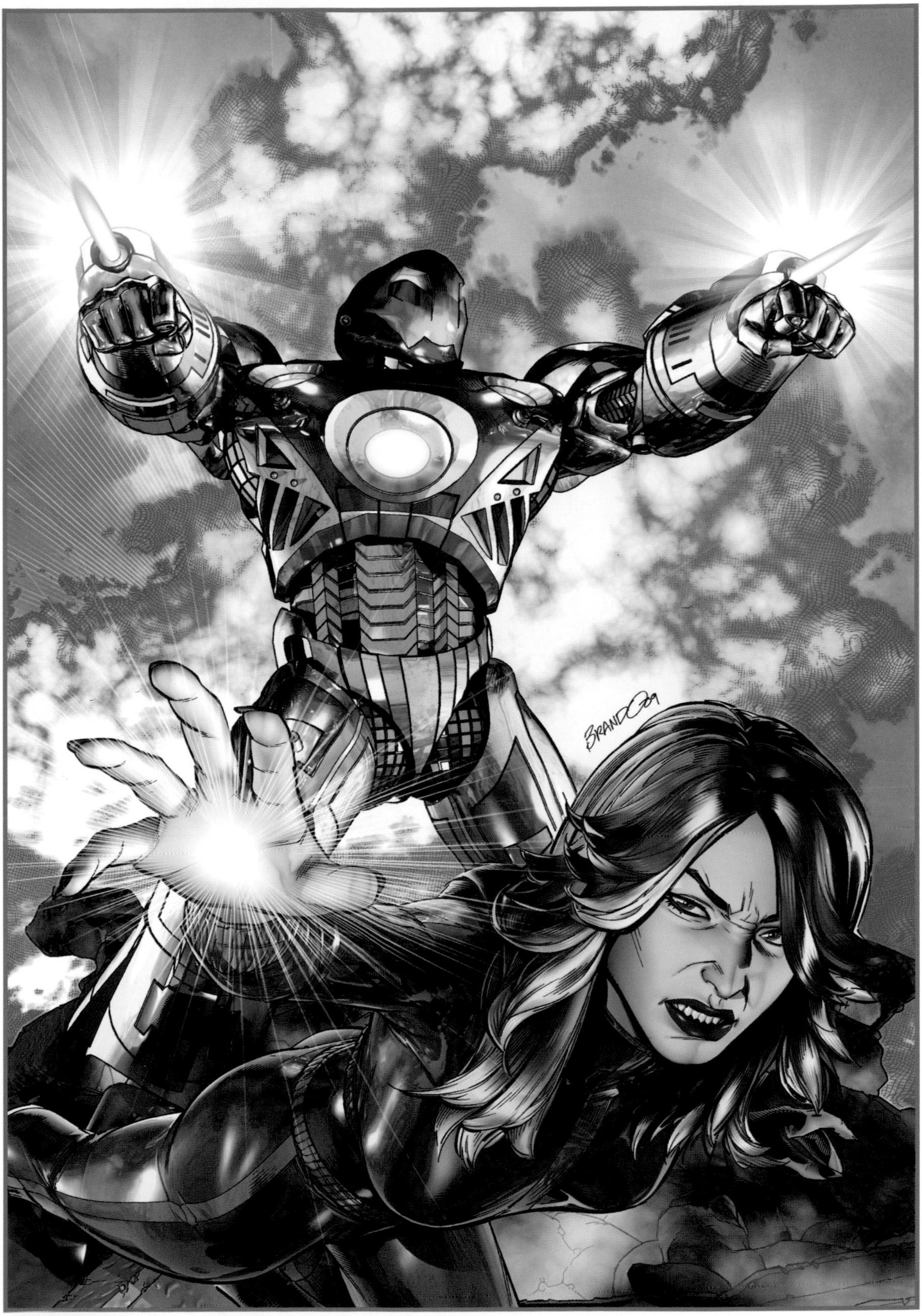

MARVEL®

ISSUE 002 COVER

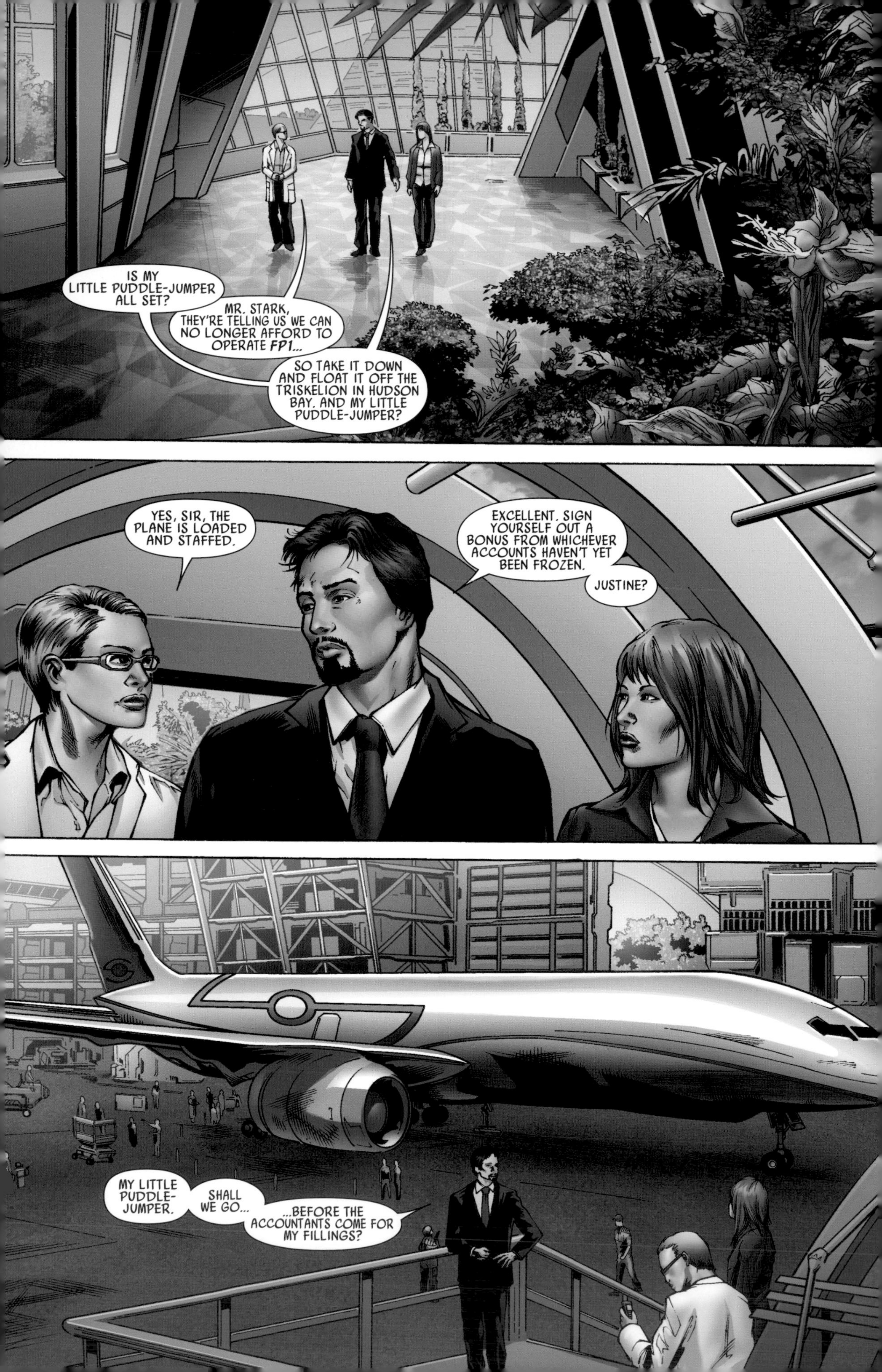

IS MY LITTLE PUDDLE-JUMPER ALL SET?
MR. STARK, THEY'RE TELLING US WE CAN NO LONGER AFFORD TO OPERATE *FP1*...
SO TAKE IT DOWN AND FLOAT IT OFF THE TRISKELION IN HUDSON BAY. AND MY LITTLE PUDDLE-JUMPER?
YES, SIR, THE PLANE IS LOADED AND STAFFED.
EXCELLENT. SIGN YOURSELF OUT A BONUS FROM WHICHEVER ACCOUNTS HAVEN'T YET BEEN FROZEN.
JUSTINE?
MY LITTLE PUDDLE-JUMPER.
SHALL WE GO...
...BEFORE THE ACCOUNTANTS COME FOR MY FILLINGS?

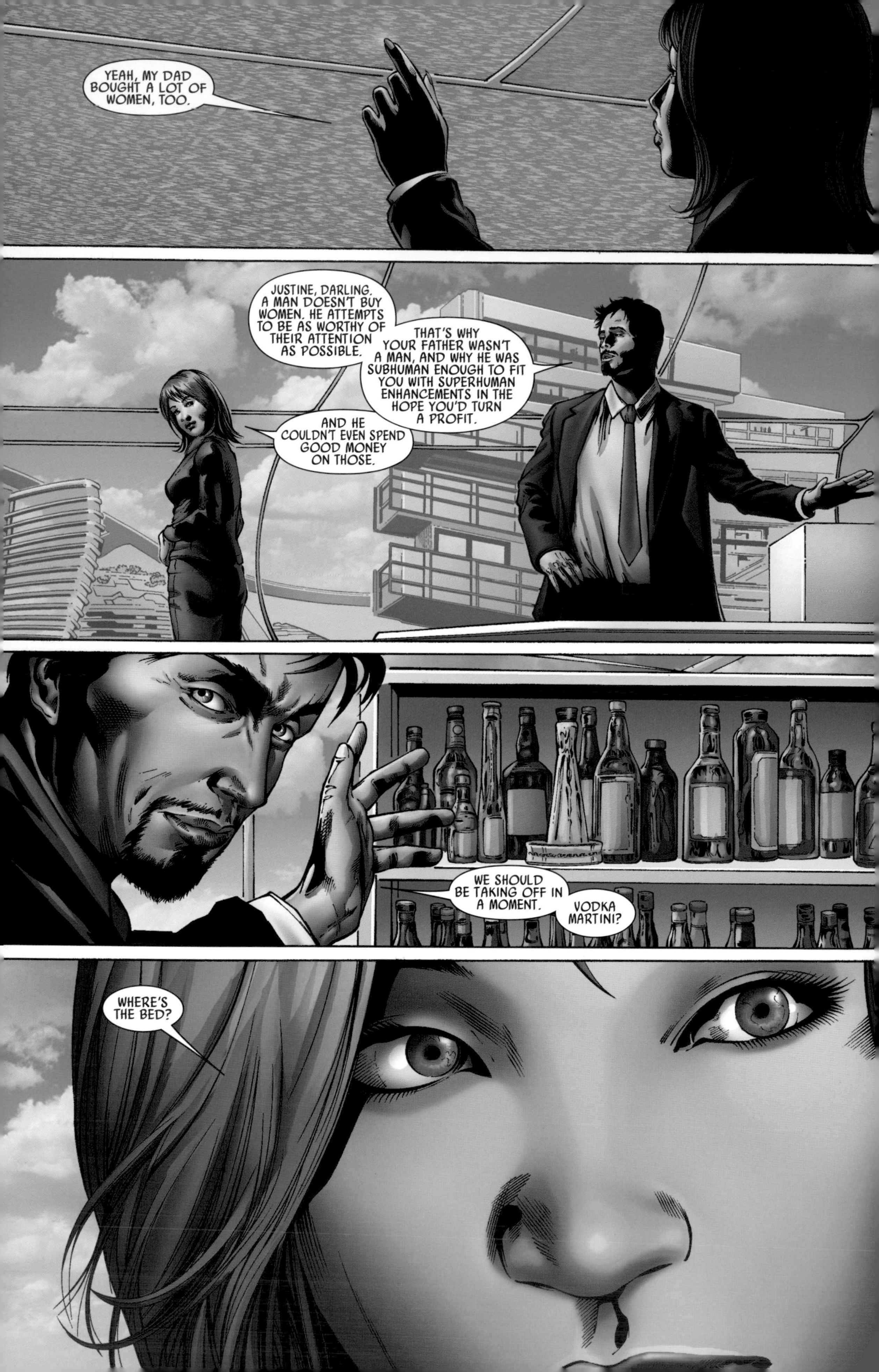
YEAH, MY DAD BOUGHT A LOT OF WOMEN, TOO.
JUSTINE, DARLING. A MAN DOESN'T BUY WOMEN. HE ATTEMPTS TO BE AS WORTHY OF THEIR ATTENTION AS POSSIBLE.
THAT'S WHY YOUR FATHER WASN'T A MAN, AND WHY HE WAS SUBHUMAN ENOUGH TO FIT YOU WITH SUPERHUMAN ENHANCEMENTS IN THE HOPE YOU'D TURN A PROFIT.
AND HE COULDN'T EVEN SPEND GOOD MONEY ON THOSE.
WE SHOULD BE TAKING OFF IN A MOMENT.
VODKA MARTINI?
WHERE'S THE BED?

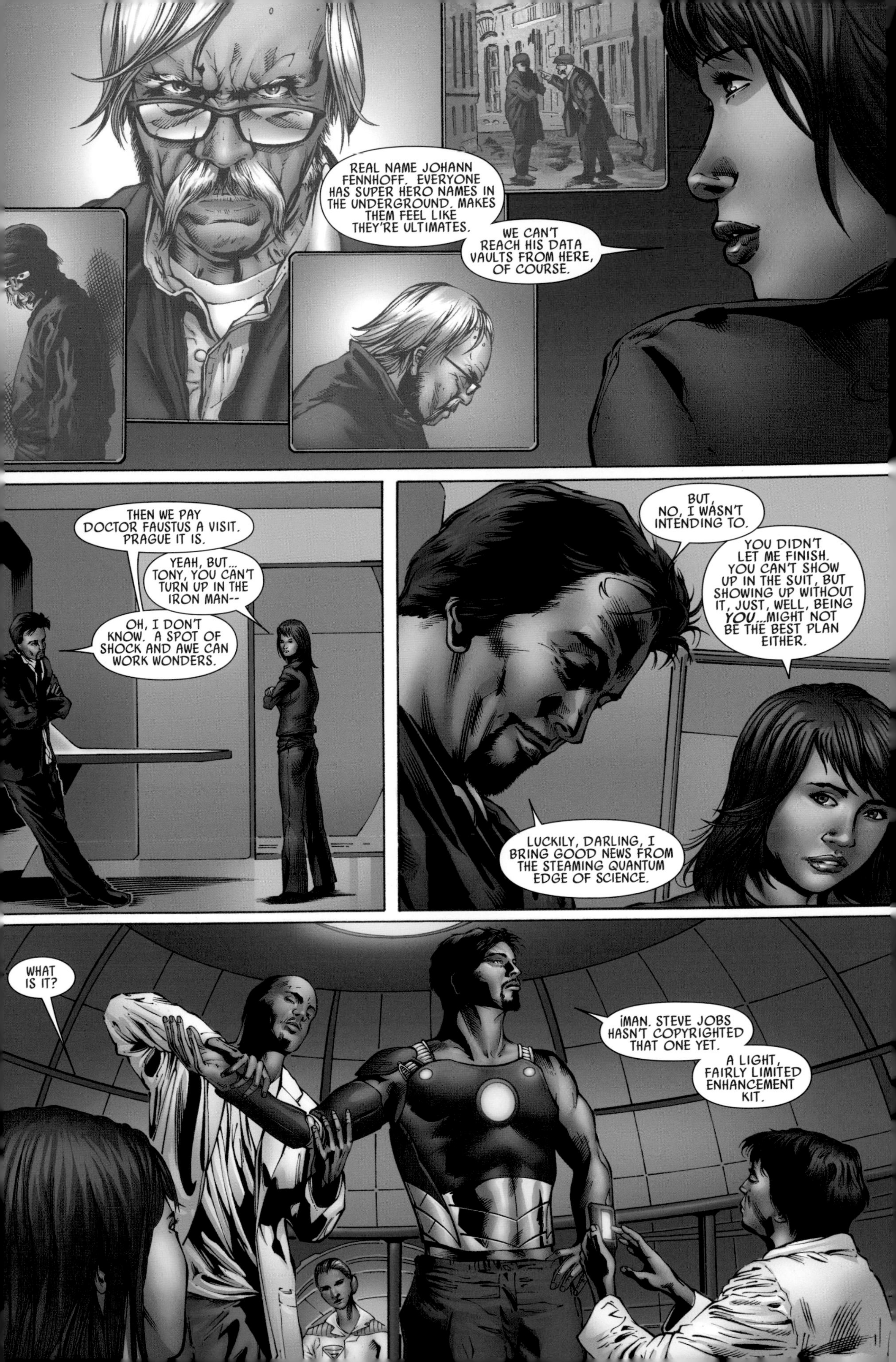
REAL NAME JOHANN FENNHOFF. EVERYONE HAS SUPER HERO NAMES IN THE UNDERGROUND. MAKES THEM FEEL LIKE THEY'RE ULTIMATES.
WE CAN'T REACH HIS DATA VAULTS FROM HERE, OF COURSE.
THEN WE PAY DOCTOR FAUSTUS A VISIT. PRAGUE IT IS.
YEAH, BUT... TONY, YOU CAN'T TURN UP IN THE IRON MAN--
OH, I DON'T KNOW. A SPOT OF SHOCK AND AWE CAN WORK WONDERS.
BUT, NO, I WASN'T INTENDING TO.
YOU DIDN'T LET ME FINISH. YOU CAN'T SHOW UP IN THE SUIT, BUT SHOWING UP WITHOUT IT, JUST, WELL, BEING *YOU*...MIGHT NOT BE THE BEST PLAN EITHER.
LUCKILY, DARLING, I BRING GOOD NEWS FROM THE STEAMING QUANTUM EDGE OF SCIENCE.
WHAT IS IT?
iMAN. STEVE JOBS HASN'T COPYRIGHTED THAT ONE YET.
A LIGHT, FAIRLY LIMITED ENHANCEMENT KIT.

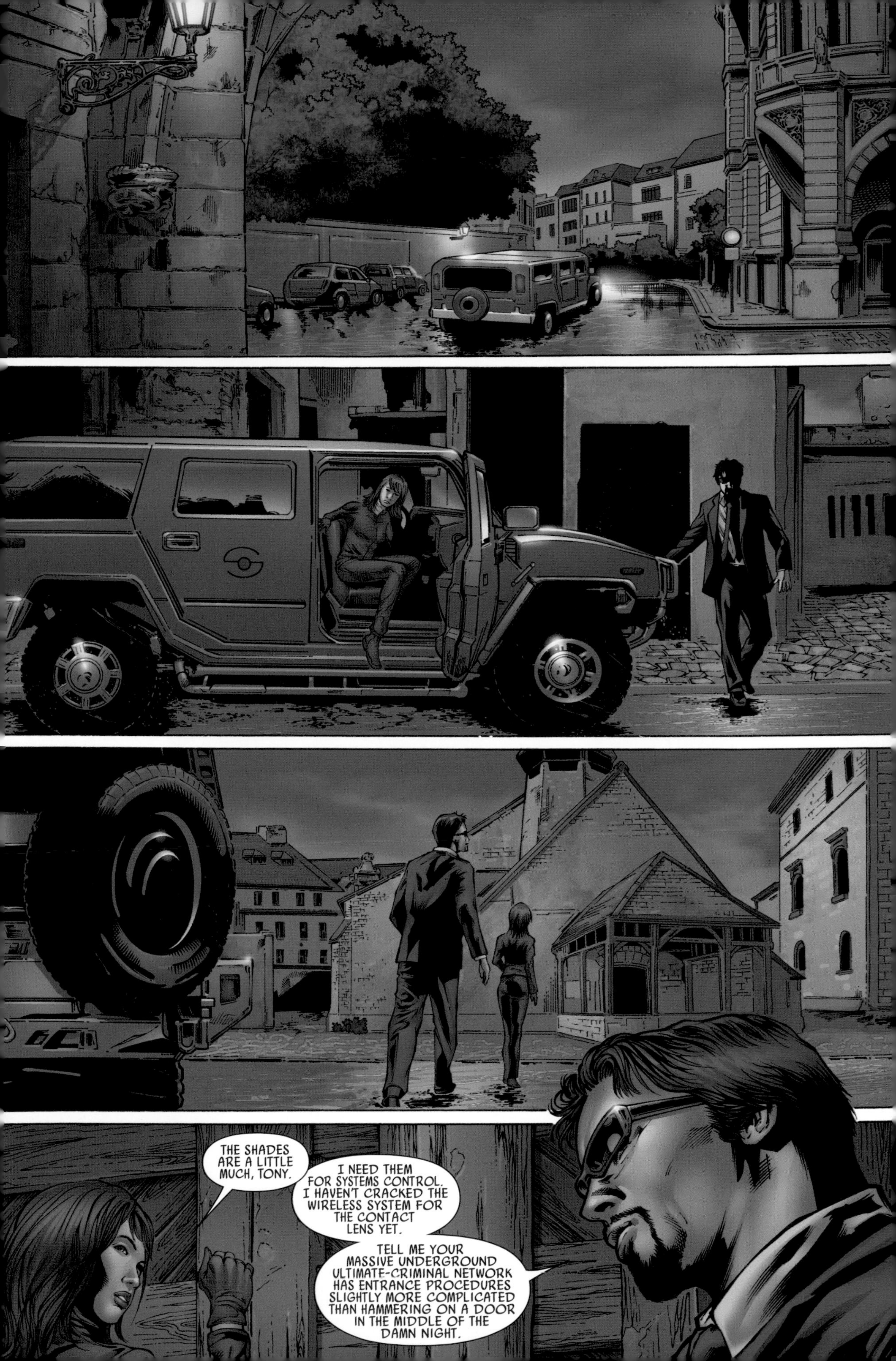

THE SHADES ARE A LITTLE MUCH, TONY.
I NEED THEM FOR SYSTEMS CONTROL. I HAVEN'T CRACKED THE WIRELESS SYSTEM FOR THE CONTACT LENS YET.
TELL ME YOUR MASSIVE UNDERGROUND ULTIMATE-CRIMINAL NETWORK HAS ENTRANCE PROCEDURES SLIGHTLY MORE COMPLICATED THAN HAMMERING ON A DOOR IN THE MIDDLE OF THE DAMN NIGHT.

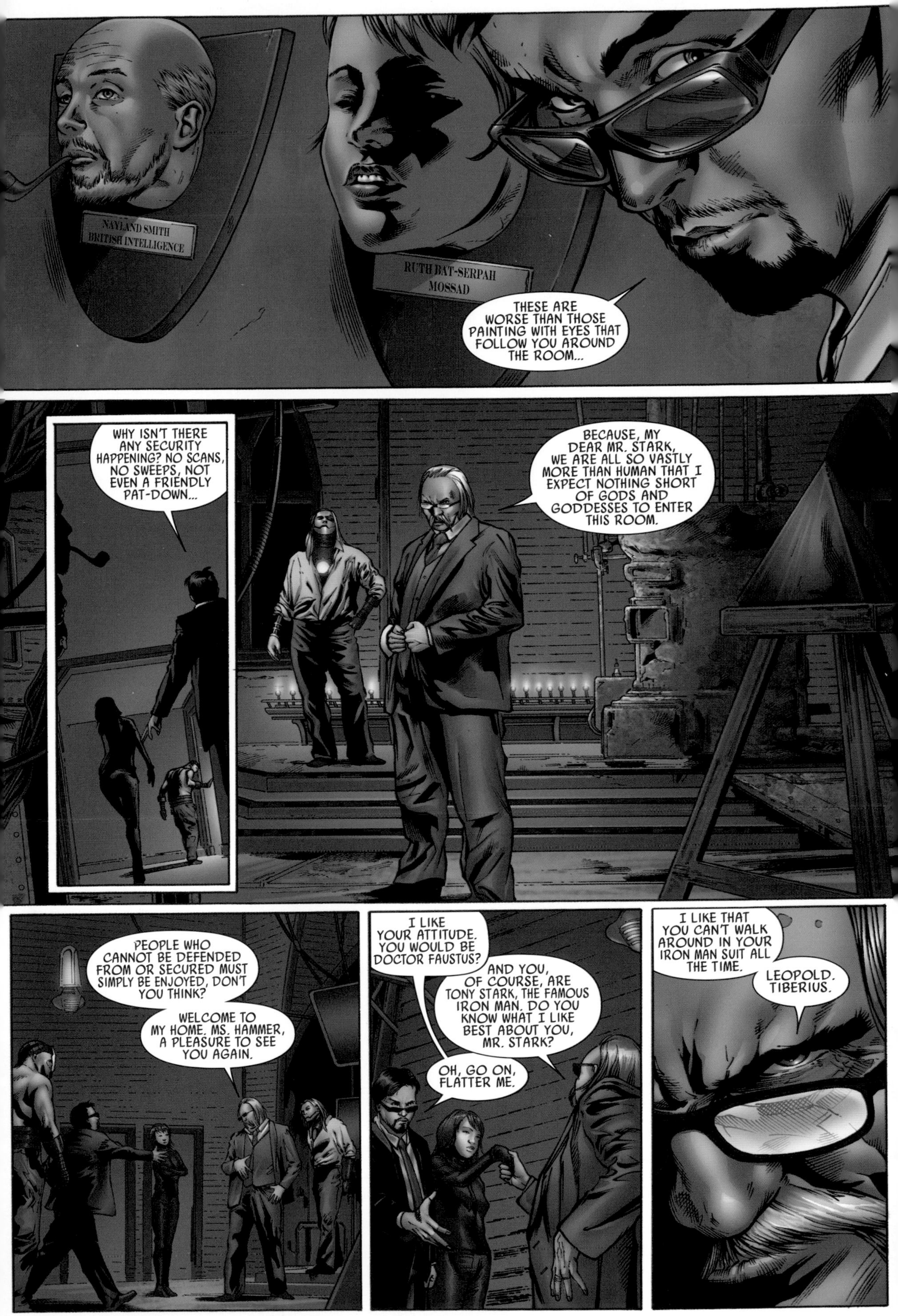
NAYLAND SMITH
BRITISH INTELLIGENCE
RUTH BAT-SERPAH
MOSSAD
THESE ARE WORSE THAN THOSE PAINTING WITH EYES THAT FOLLOW YOU AROUND THE ROOM...
WHY ISN'T THERE ANY SECURITY HAPPENING? NO SCANS, NO SWEEPS, NOT EVEN A FRIENDLY PAT-DOWN...
BECAUSE, MY DEAR MR. STARK, WE ARE ALL SO VASTLY MORE THAN HUMAN THAT I EXPECT NOTHING SHORT OF GODS AND GODDESSES TO ENTER THIS ROOM.
PEOPLE WHO CANNOT BE DEFENDED FROM OR SECURED MUST SIMPLY BE ENJOYED, DON'T YOU THINK?
WELCOME TO MY HOME. MS. HAMMER, A PLEASURE TO SEE YOU AGAIN.
I LIKE YOUR ATTITUDE. YOU WOULD BE DOCTOR FAUSTUS?
AND YOU, OF COURSE, ARE TONY STARK, THE FAMOUS IRON MAN. DO YOU KNOW WHAT I LIKE BEST ABOUT YOU, MR. STARK?
OH, GO ON, FLATTER ME.
I LIKE THAT YOU CAN'T WALK AROUND IN YOUR IRON MAN SUIT ALL THE TIME.
LEOPOLD. TIBERIUS.

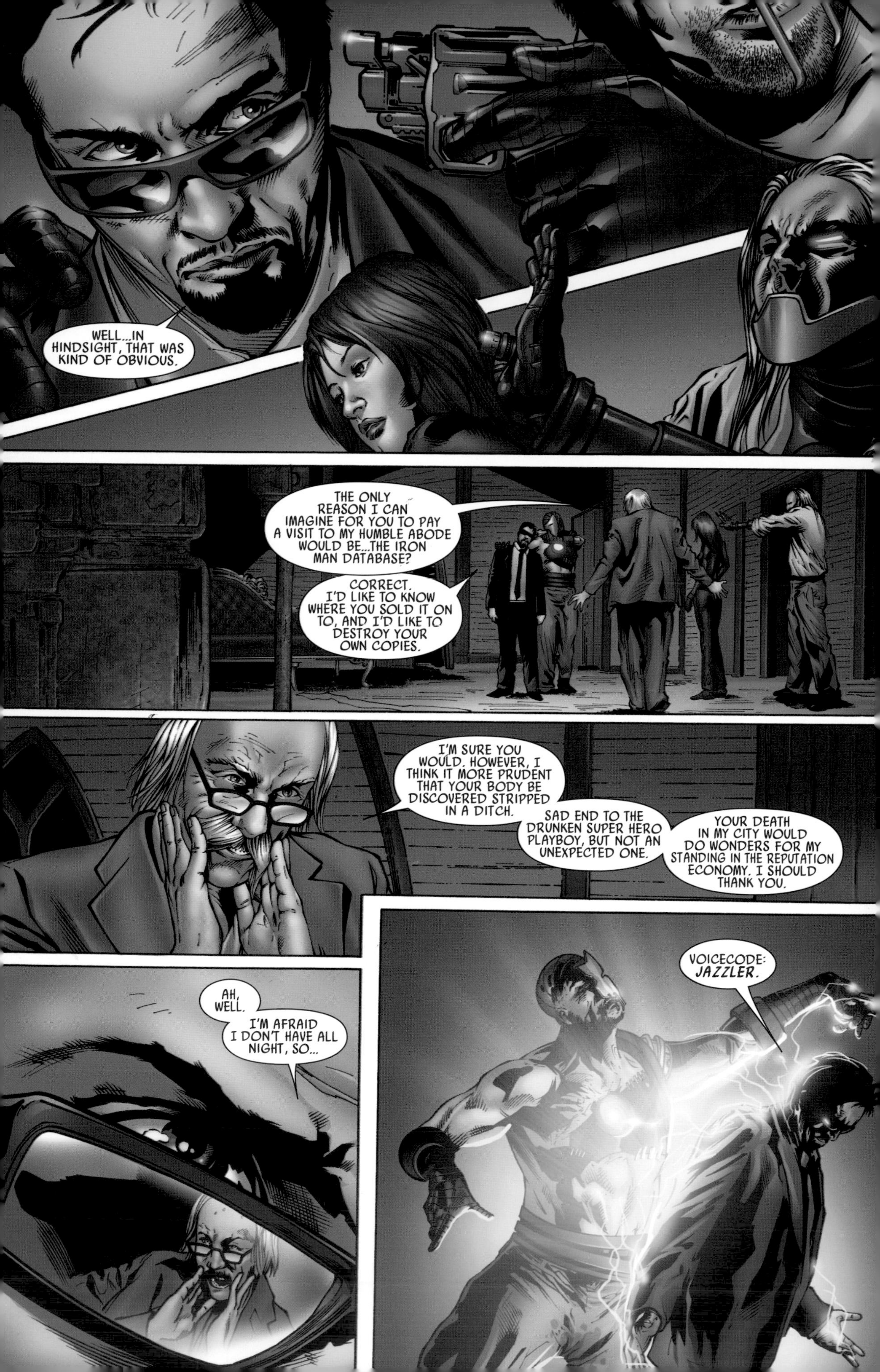
WELL...IN HINDSIGHT, THAT WAS KIND OF OBVIOUS.
THE ONLY REASON I CAN IMAGINE FOR YOU TO PAY A VISIT TO MY HUMBLE ABODE WOULD BE...THE IRON MAN DATABASE?
CORRECT. I'D LIKE TO KNOW WHERE YOU SOLD IT ON TO, AND I'D LIKE TO DESTROY YOUR OWN COPIES.
I'M SURE YOU WOULD. HOWEVER, I THINK IT MORE PRUDENT THAT YOUR BODY BE DISCOVERED STRIPPED IN A DITCH.
SAD END TO THE DRUNKEN SUPER HERO PLAYBOY, BUT NOT AN UNEXPECTED ONE.
YOUR DEATH IN MY CITY WOULD DO WONDERS FOR MY STANDING IN THE REPUTATION ECONOMY. I SHOULD THANK YOU.
AH, WELL.
I'M AFRAID I DON'T HAVE ALL NIGHT, SO...
VOICECODE: JAZZLER.

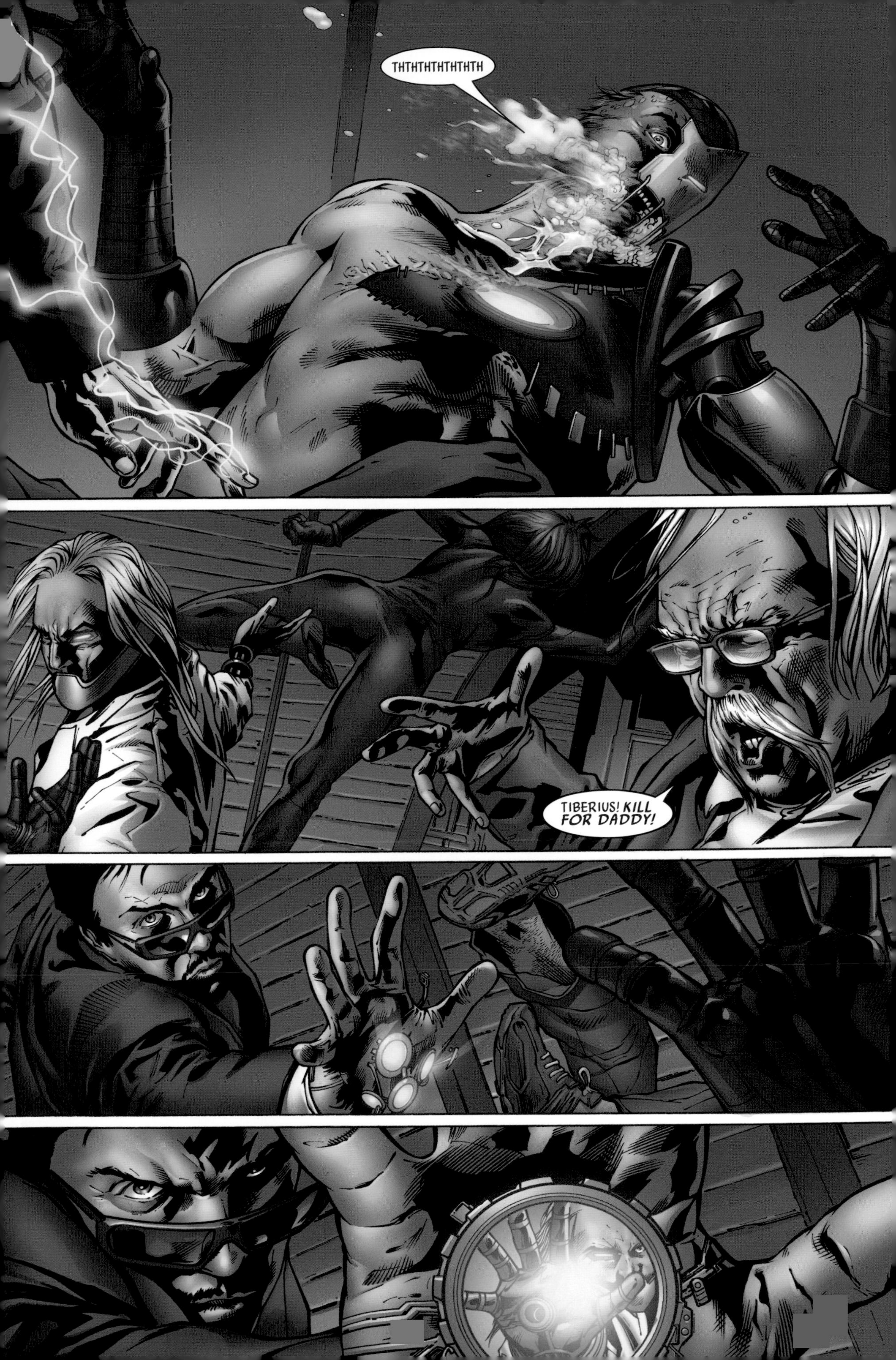
THTHTHTHTHTHTH
TIBERIUS! KILL FOR DADDY!

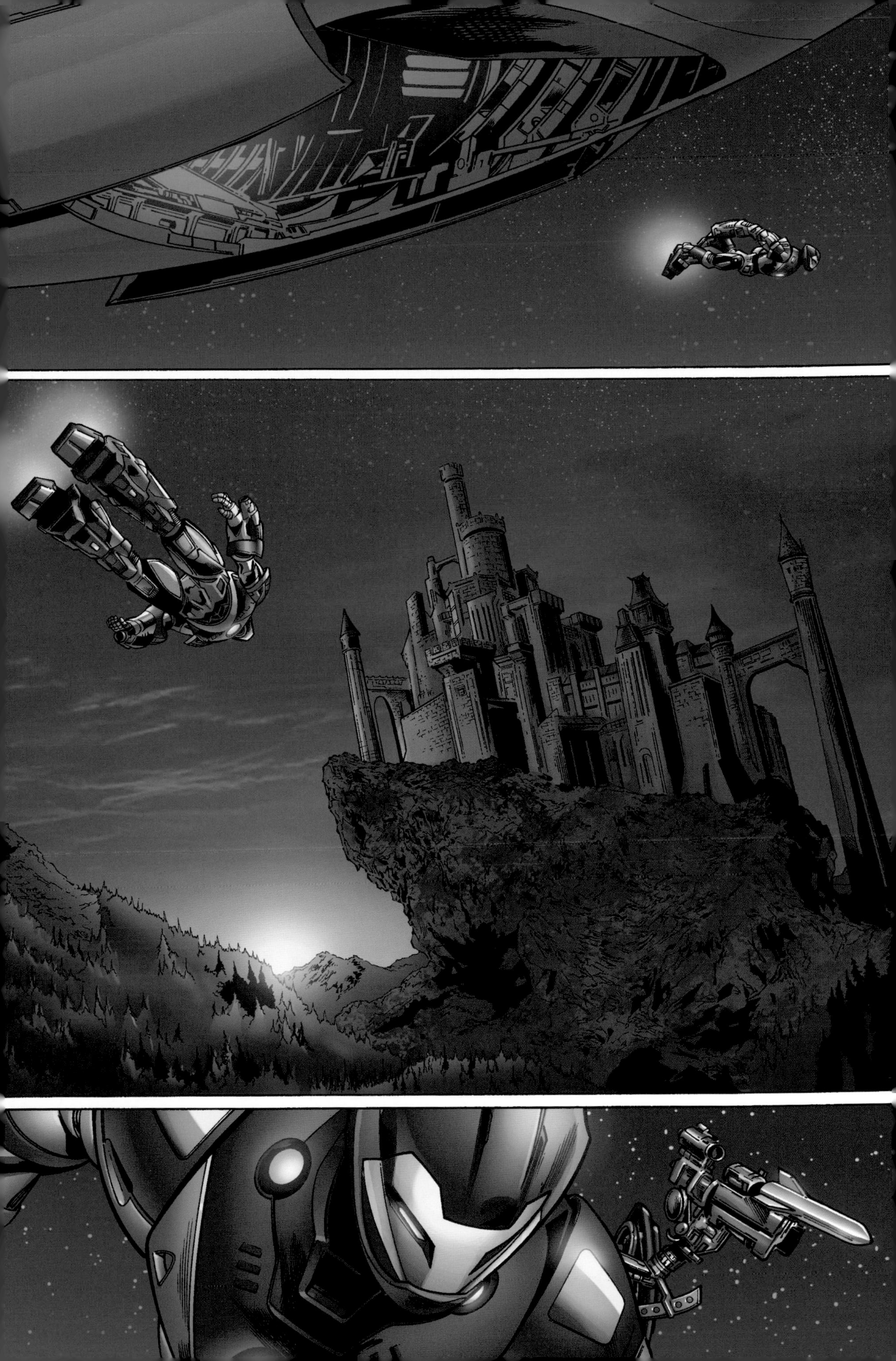

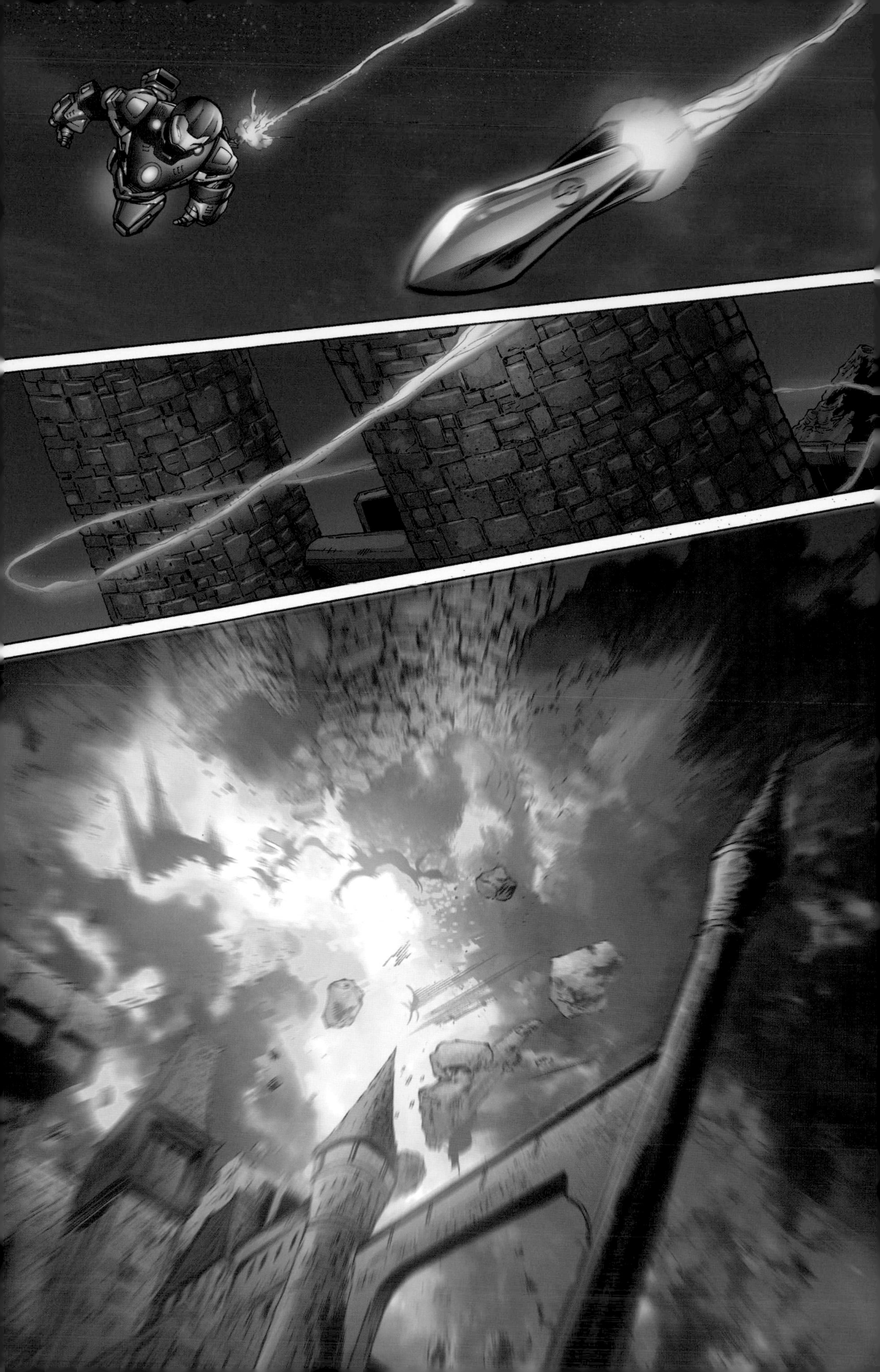

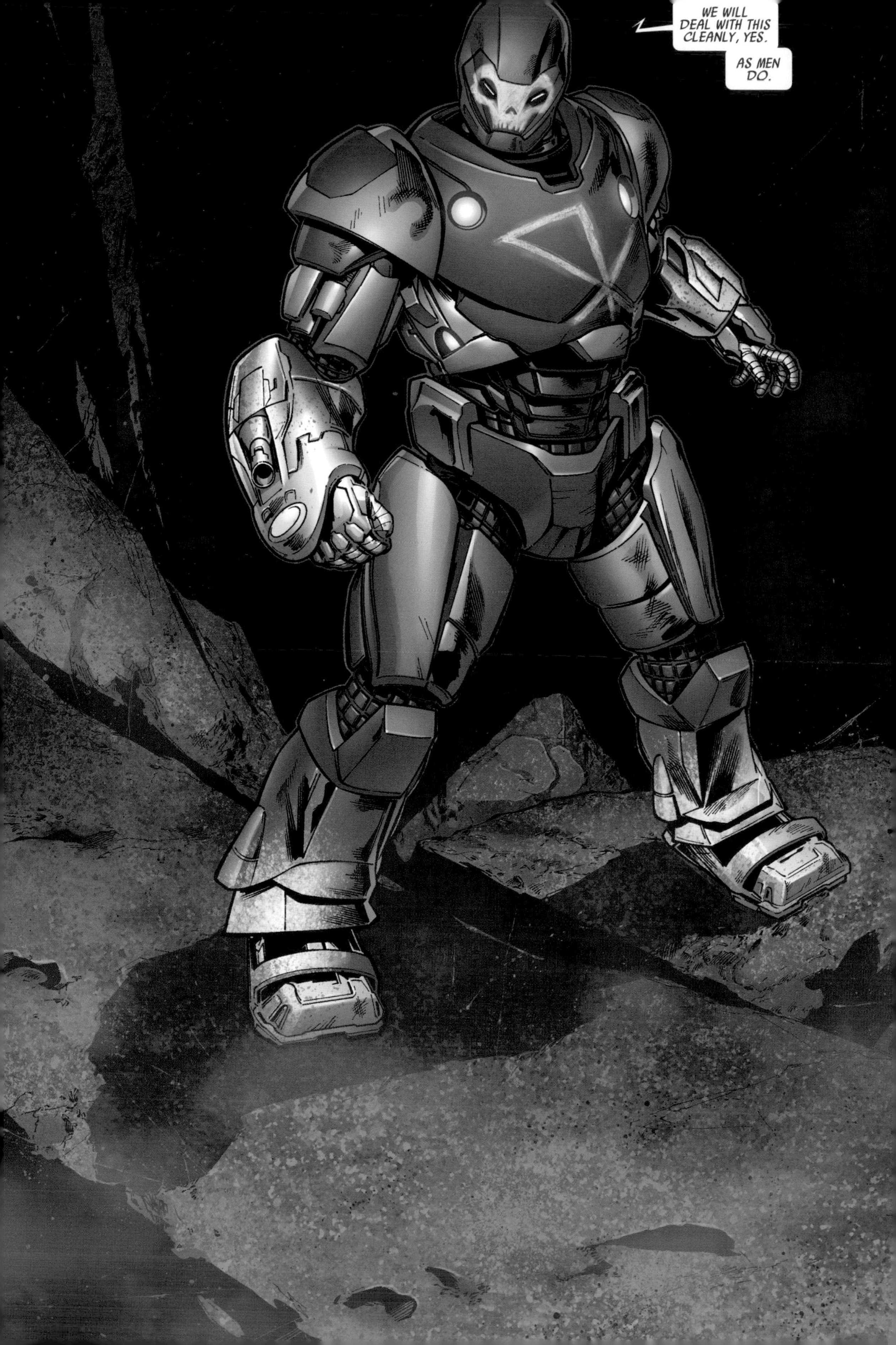
WE WILL DEAL WITH THIS CLEANLY, YES.
AS MEN DO.

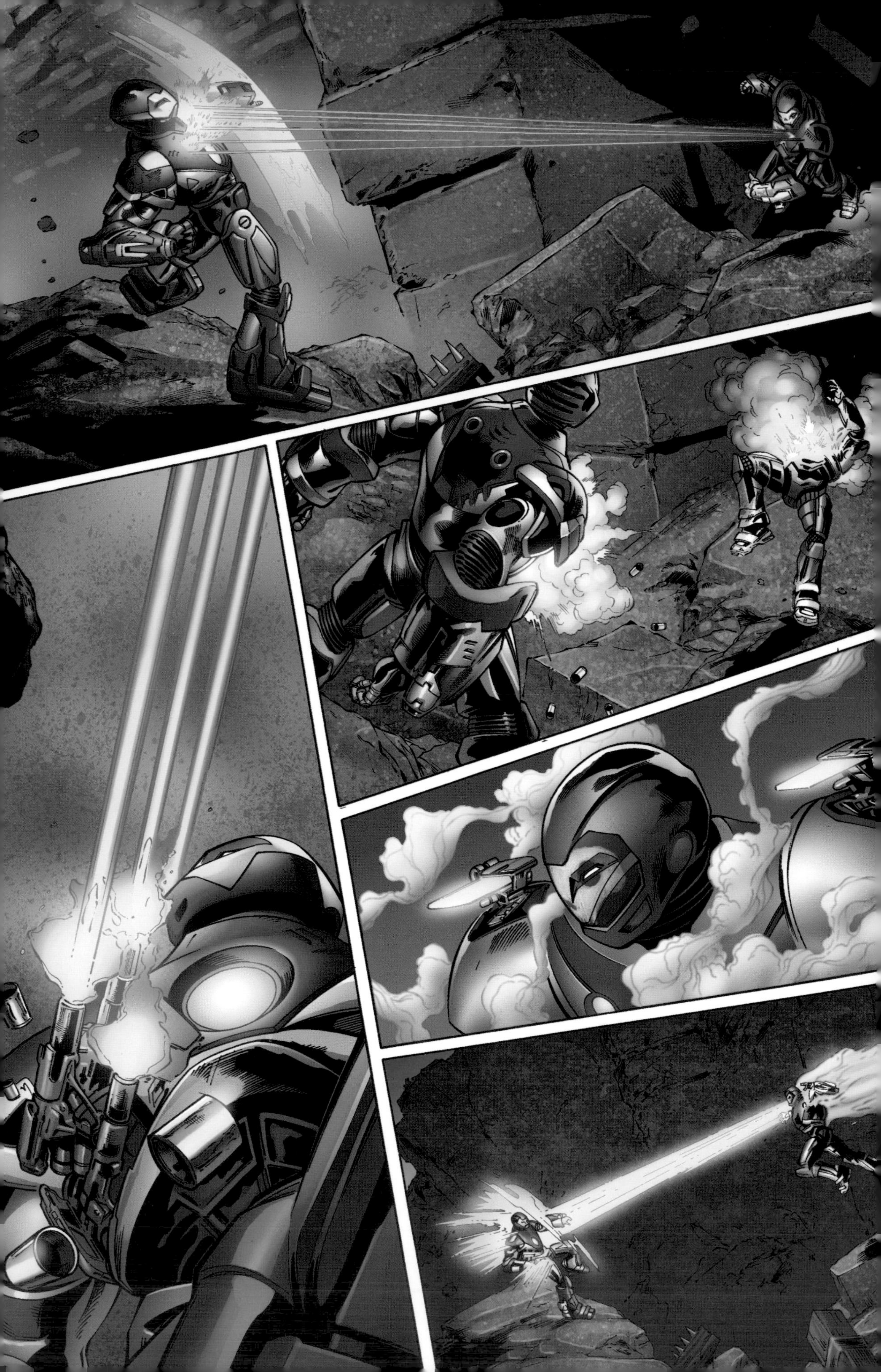

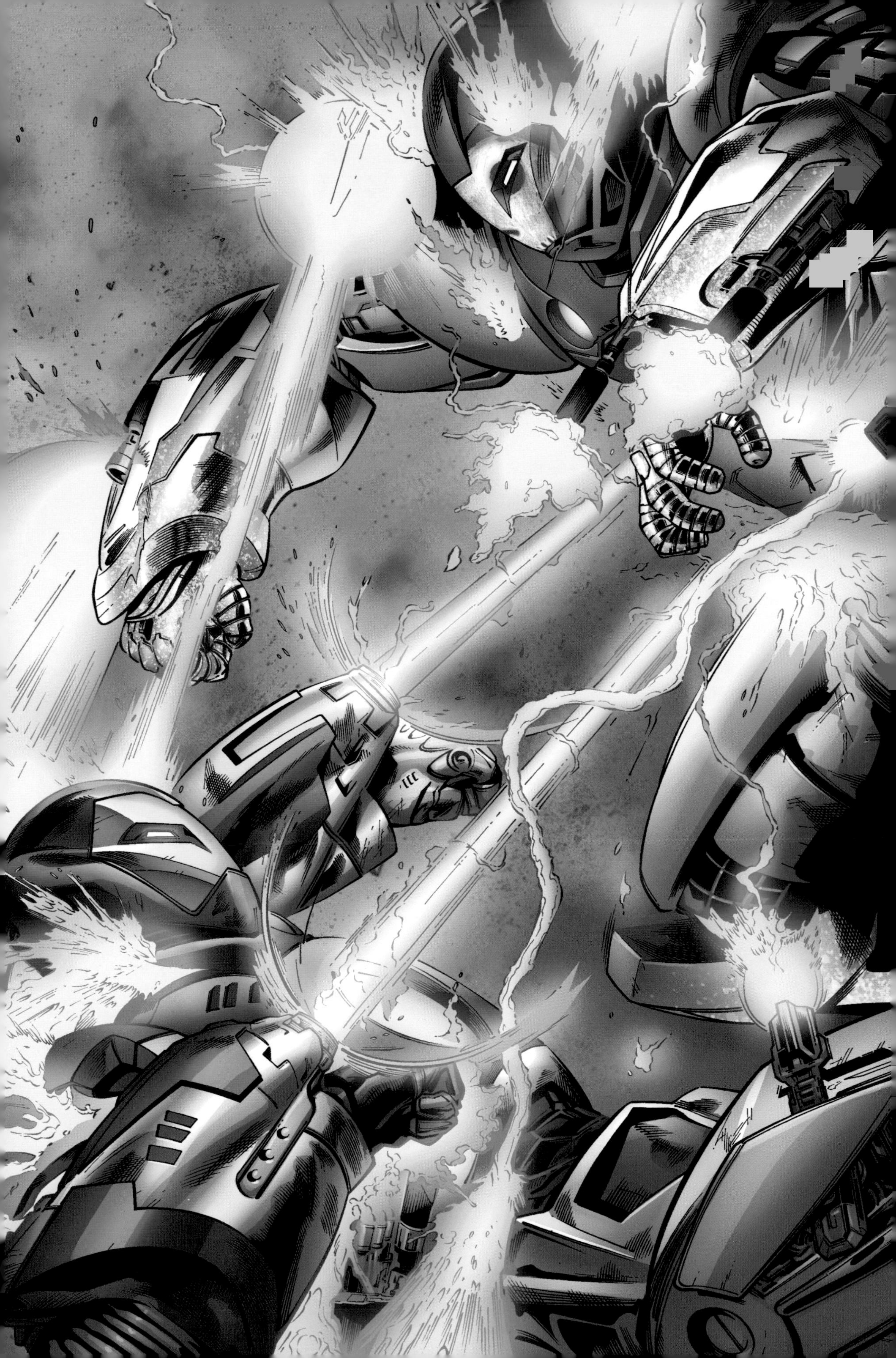

ARMOUR WARS

ULTIMATE

ISSUE 003 COVER

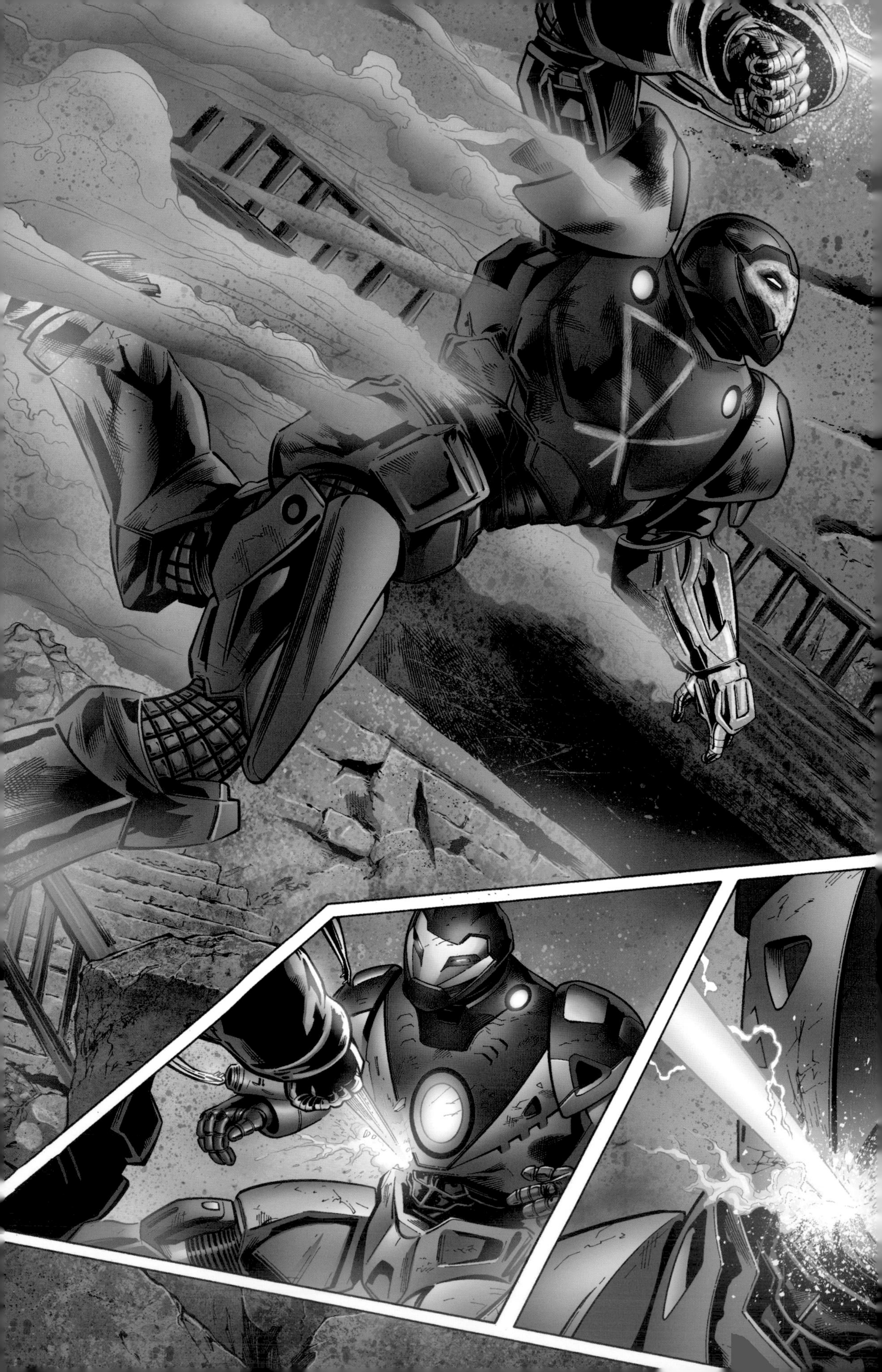

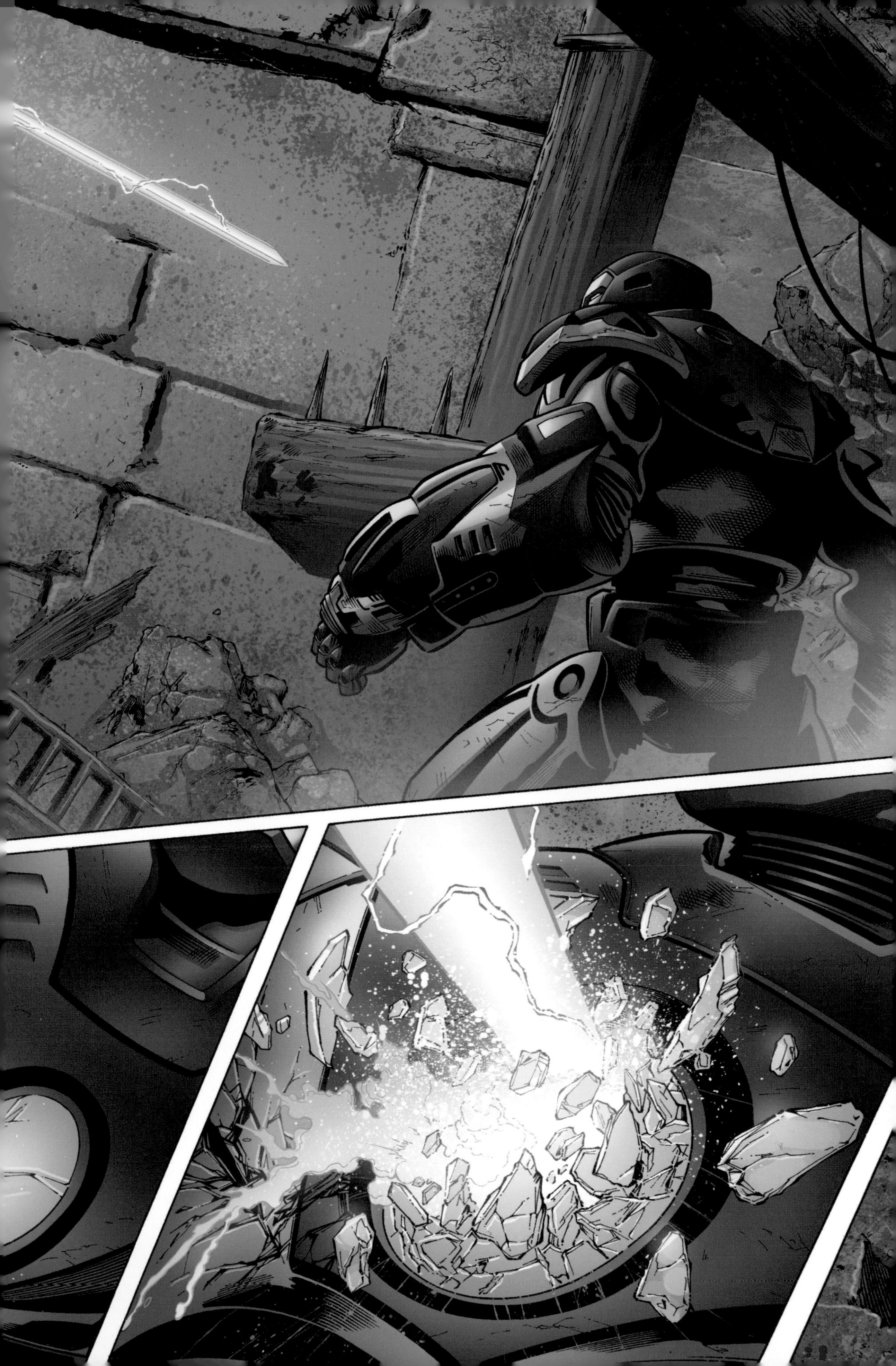

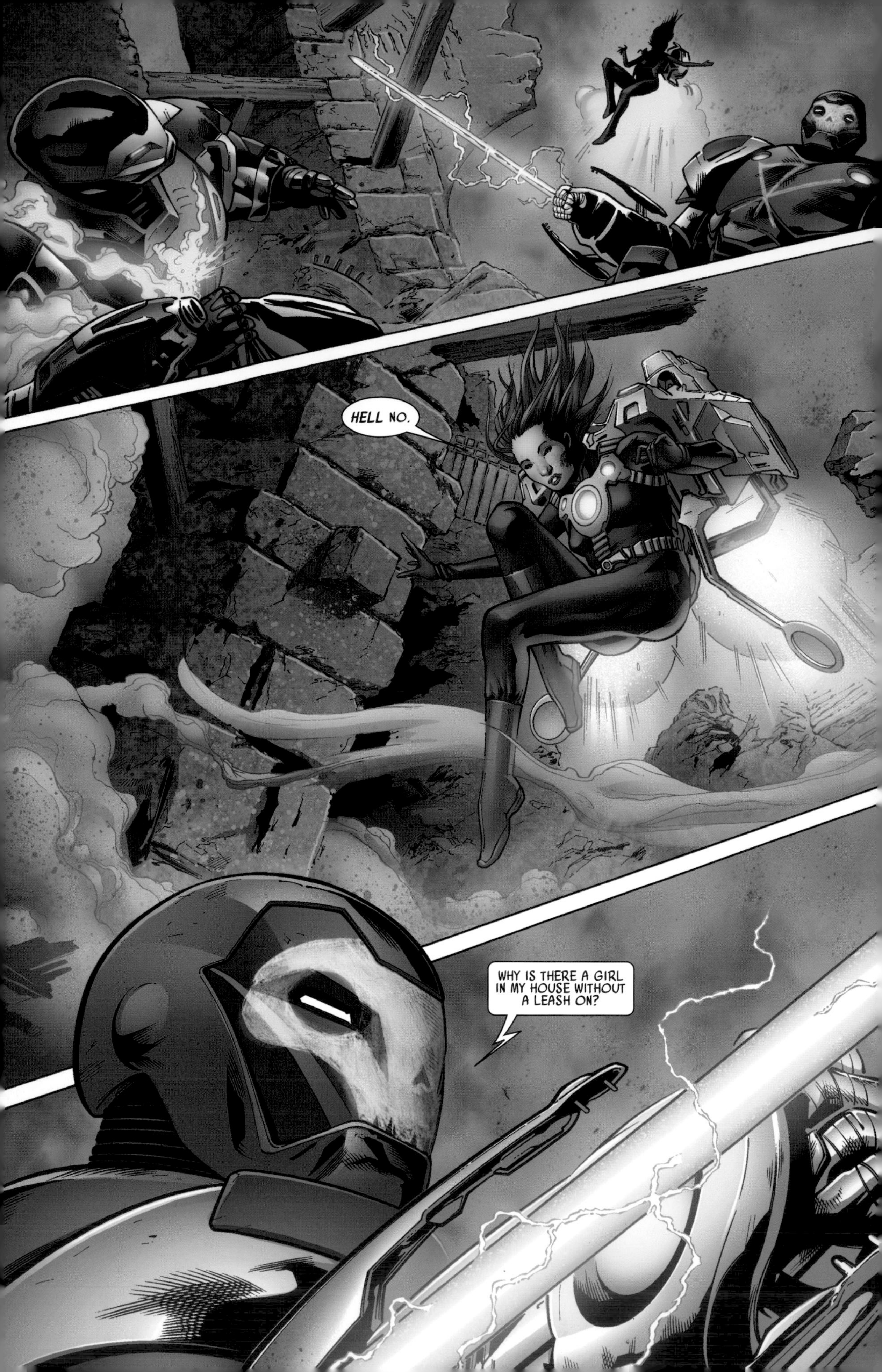
HELL NO.
WHY IS THERE A GIRL IN MY HOUSE WITHOUT A LEASH ON?

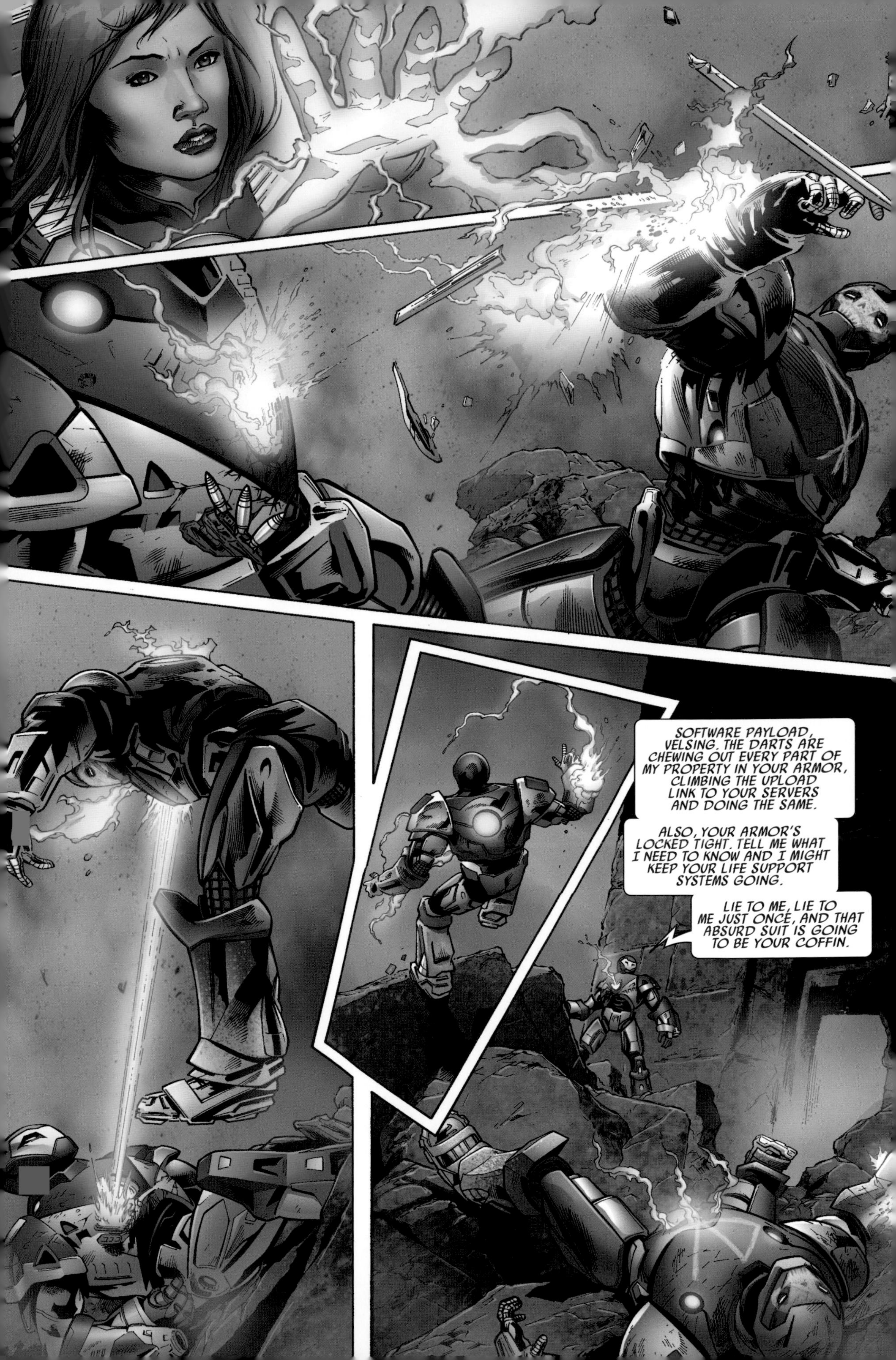
SOFTWARE PAYLOAD, VELSING. THE DARTS ARE CHEWING OUT EVERY PART OF MY PROPERTY IN YOUR ARMOR, CLIMBING THE UPLOAD LINK TO YOUR SERVERS AND DOING THE SAME.
ALSO, YOUR ARMOR'S LOCKED TIGHT. TELL ME WHAT I NEED TO KNOW AND I MIGHT KEEP YOUR LIFE SUPPORT SYSTEMS GOING.
LIE TO ME, LIE TO ME JUST ONCE, AND THAT ABSURD SUIT IS GOING TO BE YOUR COFFIN.

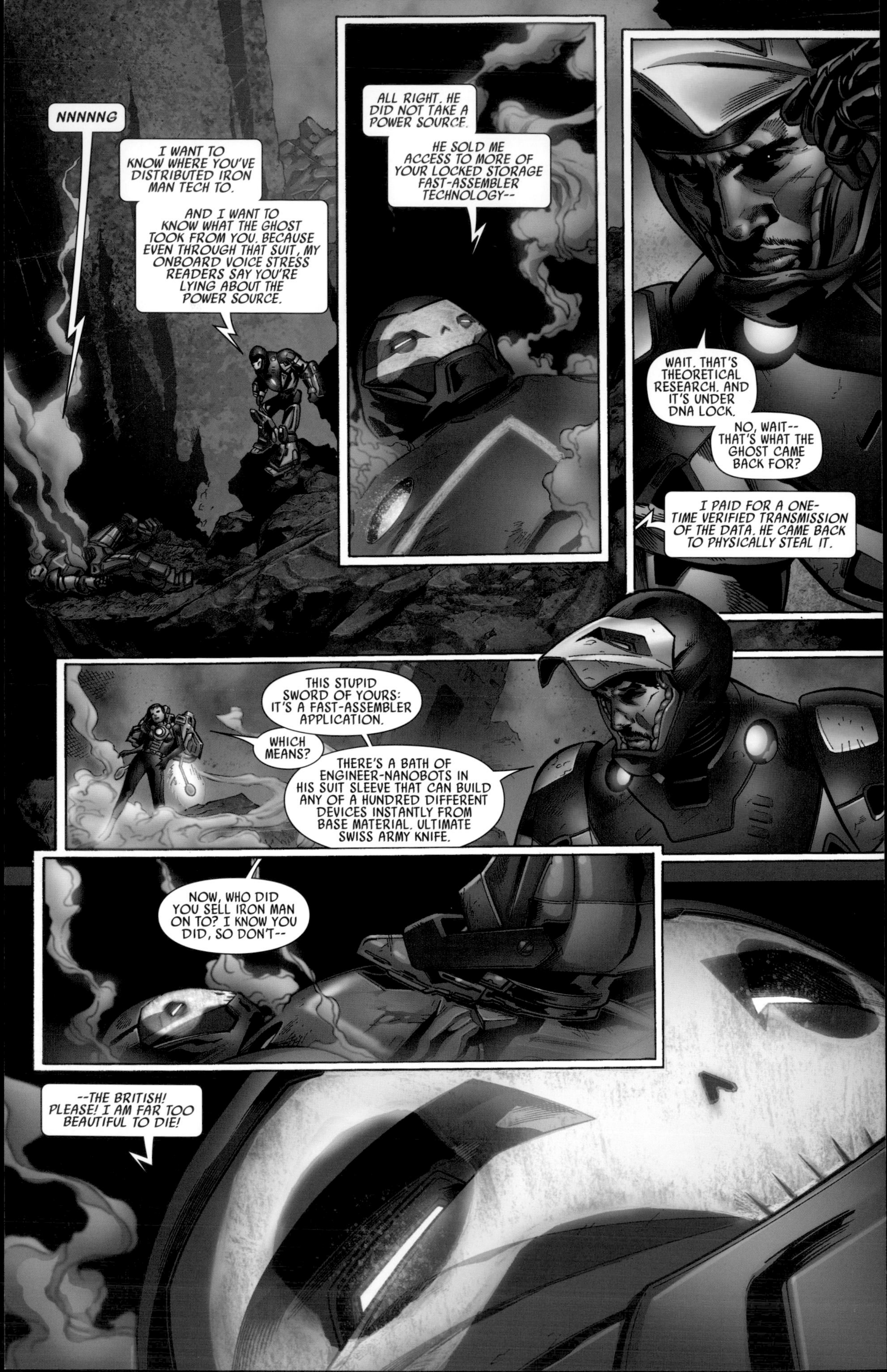
NNNNNG
I WANT TO KNOW WHERE YOU'VE DISTRIBUTED IRON MAN TECH TO.
AND I WANT TO KNOW WHAT THE GHOST TOOK FROM YOU. BECAUSE EVEN THROUGH THAT SUIT, MY ONBOARD VOICE STRESS READERS SAY YOU'RE LYING ABOUT THE POWER SOURCE.
ALL RIGHT. HE DID NOT TAKE A POWER SOURCE.
HE SOLD ME ACCESS TO MORE OF YOUR LOCKED STORAGE FAST-ASSEMBLER TECHNOLOGY--
WAIT. THAT'S THEORETICAL RESEARCH. AND IT'S UNDER DNA LOCK.
NO, WAIT-- THAT'S WHAT THE GHOST CAME BACK FOR?
I PAID FOR A ONE-TIME VERIFIED TRANSMISSION OF THE DATA. HE CAME BACK TO PHYSICALLY STEAL IT.
THIS STUPID SWORD OF YOURS: IT'S A FAST-ASSEMBLER APPLICATION.
WHICH MEANS?
THERE'S A BATH OF ENGINEER-NANOBOTS IN HIS SUIT SLEEVE THAT CAN BUILD ANY OF A HUNDRED DIFFERENT DEVICES INSTANTLY FROM BASE MATERIAL. ULTIMATE SWISS ARMY KNIFE.
NOW, WHO DID YOU SELL IRON MAN ON TO? I KNOW YOU DID, SO DON'T--
--THE BRITISH! PLEASE! I AM FAR TOO BEAUTIFUL TO DIE!

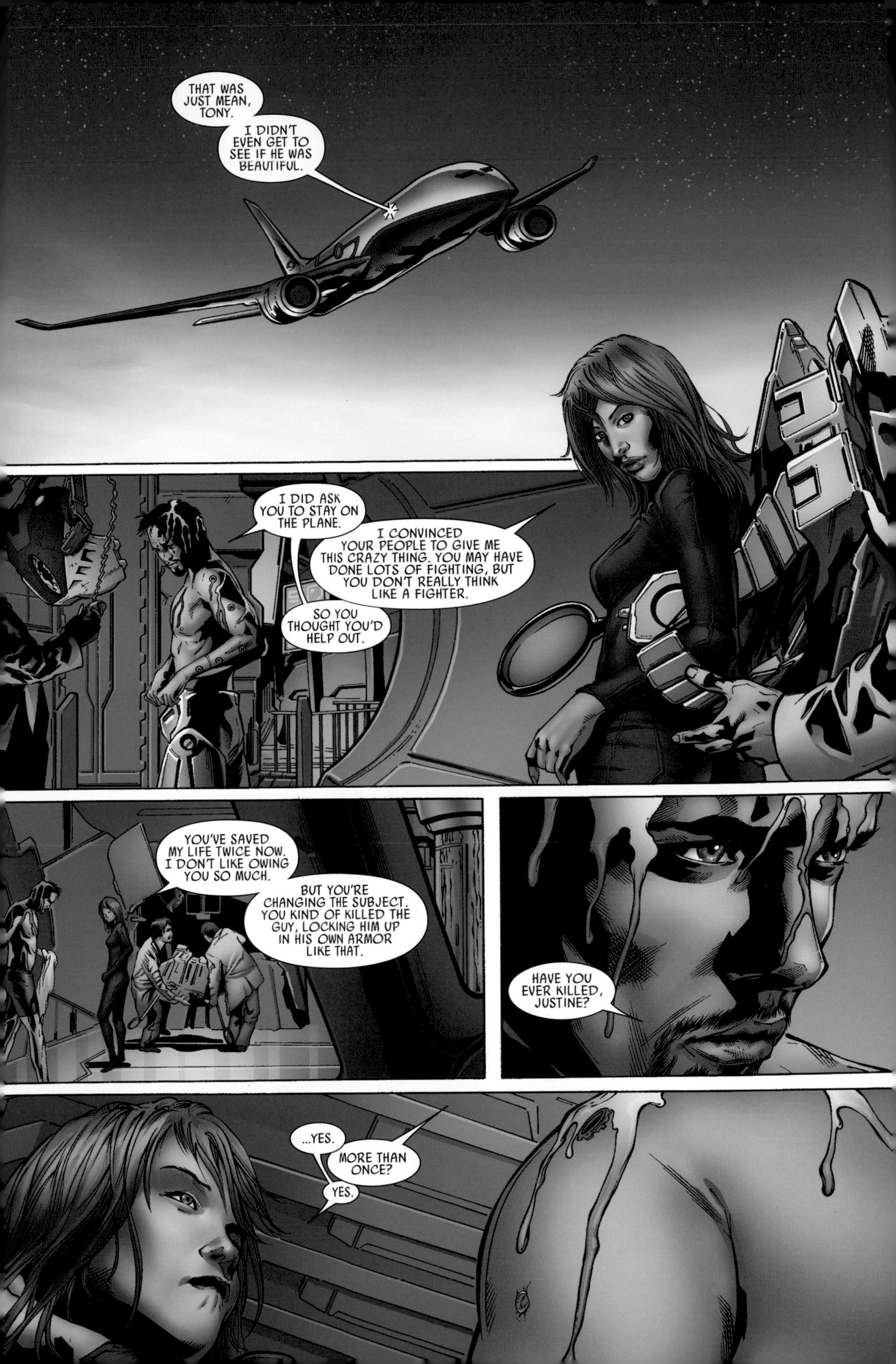
THAT WAS JUST MEAN, TONY.
I DIDN'T EVEN GET TO SEE IF HE WAS BEAUTIFUL.
I DID ASK YOU TO STAY ON THE PLANE.
I CONVINCED YOUR PEOPLE TO GIVE ME THIS CRAZY THING. YOU MAY HAVE DONE LOTS OF FIGHTING, BUT YOU DON'T REALLY THINK LIKE A FIGHTER.
SO YOU THOUGHT YOU'D HELP OUT.
YOU'VE SAVED MY LIFE TWICE NOW. I DON'T LIKE OWING YOU SO MUCH.
BUT YOU'RE CHANGING THE SUBJECT. YOU KIND OF KILLED THE GUY, LOCKING HIM UP IN HIS OWN ARMOR LIKE THAT.
HAVE YOU EVER KILLED, JUSTINE?
...YES.
MORE THAN ONCE?
YES.

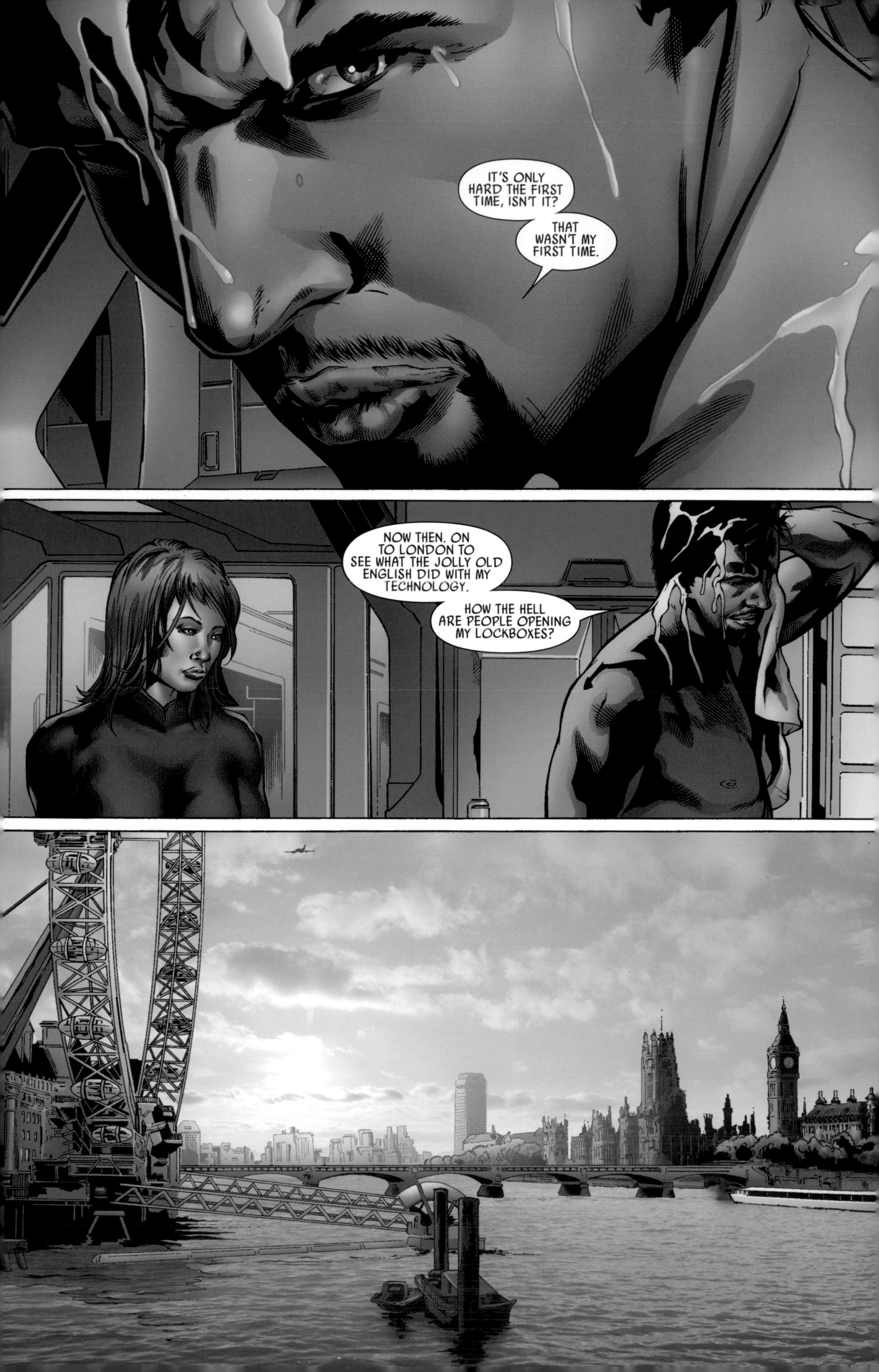

IT'S ONLY HARD THE FIRST TIME, ISN'T IT?
THAT WASN'T MY FIRST TIME.
NOW THEN. ON TO LONDON TO SEE WHAT THE JOLLY OLD ENGLISH DID WITH MY TECHNOLOGY.
HOW THE HELL ARE PEOPLE OPENING MY LOCKBOXES?

I SWEAR YOU'RE MAKING ME INTO AN ALCOHOLIC JUST LIKE YOU.

I AM NOT AN ALCOHOLIC. I SIMPLY HAVE A TERRIBLE DRINKS DEFICIENCY.

MR. STARK, YOU NEED TO SEE THIS.

CALM DOWN, JASPER. YOU'LL CLIP YEARS OFF YOUR LIFE IF YOU DON'T LEARN HOW TO--

--I AM GOING TO KILL SOMEONE.

STARKTECH ELECTROMAGNETIC SIGNATURES LIVE ON THE STREET IN LONDON.

I DO NOT BELIEVE--JUSTINE, PLEASE SWITCH THE TV TO THE BBC NEWS--

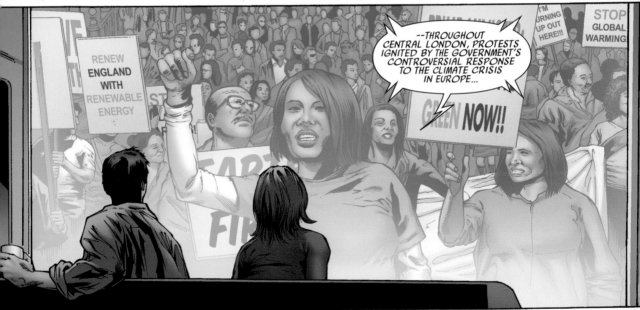

--THROUGHOUT CENTRAL LONDON, PROTESTS IGNITED BY THE GOVERNMENT'S CONTROVERSIAL RESPONSE TO THE CLIMATE CRISIS IN EUROPE...

RENEW ENGLAND WITH RENEWABLE ENERGY

STOP GLOBAL WARMING

GREEN NOW!!

ARE NOW BEING CONTAINED BY THE METROPOLITAN POLICE'S NEW ANTI-RIOT SQUAD, WHICH THE BBC HAS LEARNED IS CODENAMED OPERATION FIREPOWER--

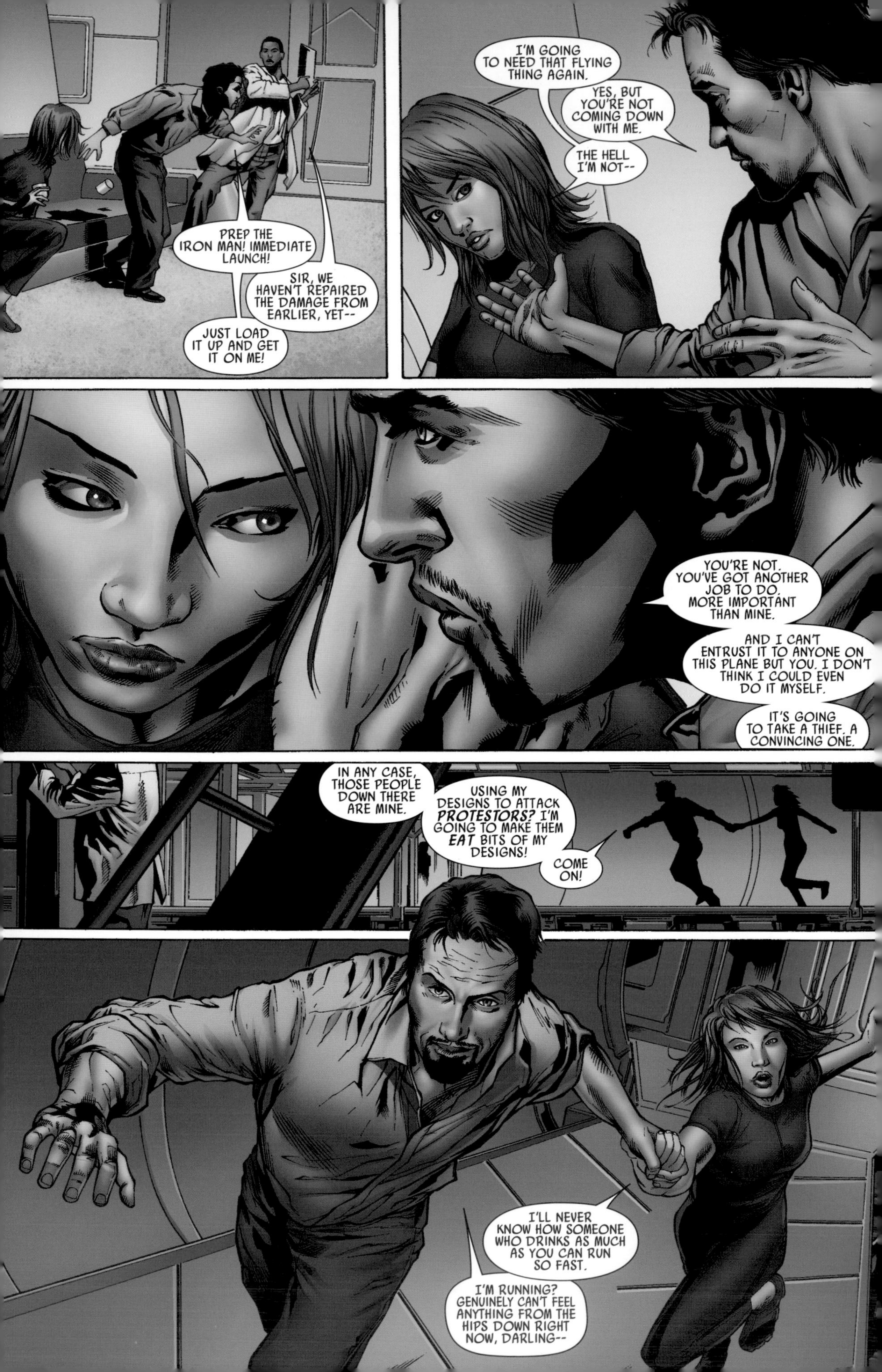
PREP THE IRON MAN! IMMEDIATE LAUNCH!
SIR, WE HAVEN'T REPAIRED THE DAMAGE FROM EARLIER, YET--
JUST LOAD IT UP AND GET IT ON ME!
I'M GOING TO NEED THAT FLYING THING AGAIN.
YES, BUT YOU'RE NOT COMING DOWN WITH ME.
THE HELL I'M NOT--
YOU'RE NOT. YOU'VE GOT ANOTHER JOB TO DO. MORE IMPORTANT THAN MINE.
AND I CAN'T ENTRUST IT TO ANYONE ON THIS PLANE BUT YOU. I DON'T THINK I COULD EVEN DO IT MYSELF.
IT'S GOING TO TAKE A THIEF. A CONVINCING ONE.
IN ANY CASE, THOSE PEOPLE DOWN THERE ARE MINE.
USING MY DESIGNS TO ATTACK *PROTESTORS?* I'M GOING TO MAKE THEM *EAT* BITS OF MY DESIGNS!
COME ON!
I'LL NEVER KNOW HOW SOMEONE WHO DRINKS AS MUCH AS YOU CAN RUN SO FAST.
I'M RUNNING? GENUINELY CAN'T FEEL ANYTHING FROM THE HIPS DOWN RIGHT NOW, DARLING--

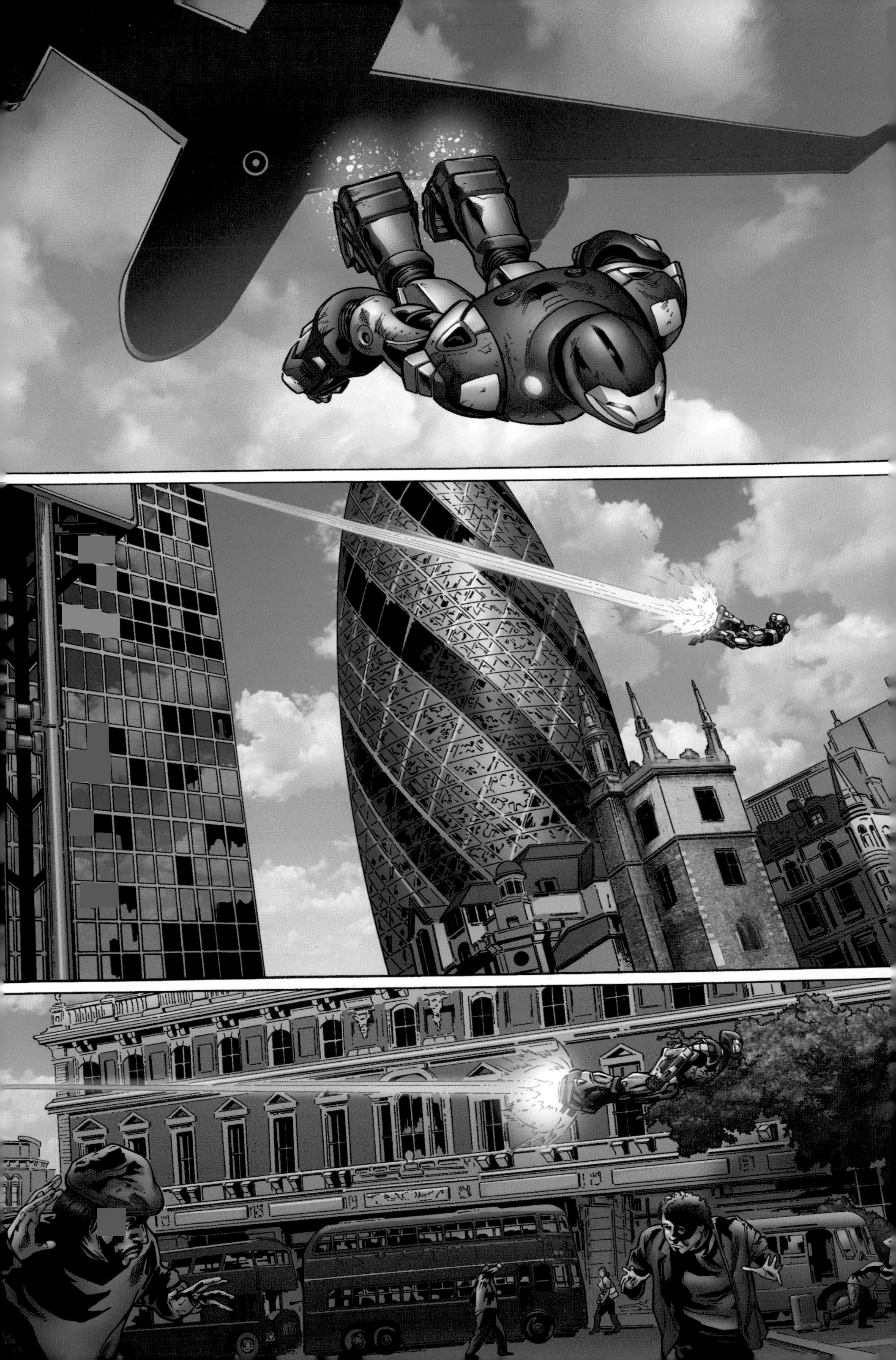

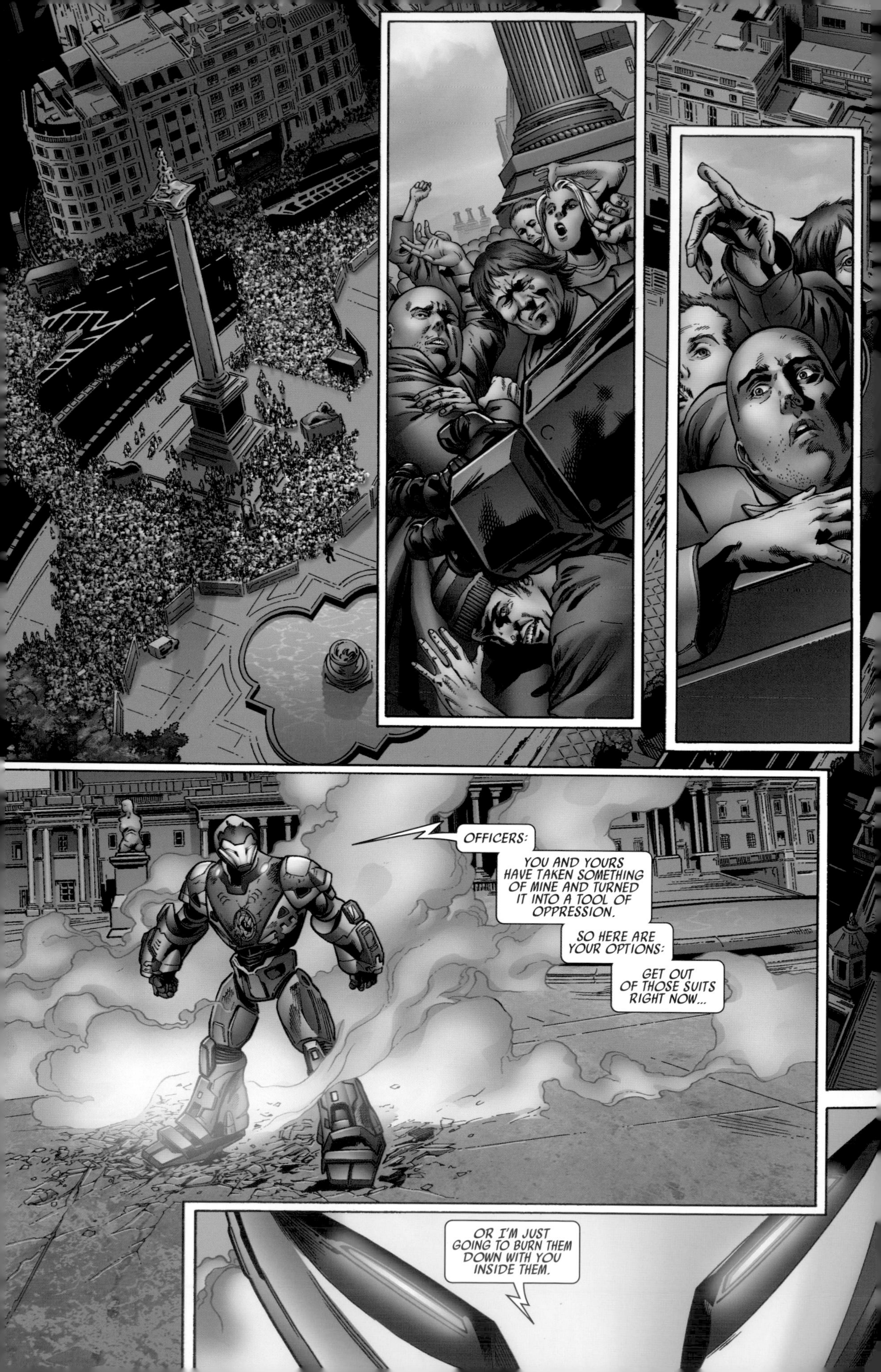

OFFICERS:
YOU AND YOURS HAVE TAKEN SOMETHING OF MINE AND TURNED IT INTO A TOOL OF OPPRESSION.
SO HERE ARE YOUR OPTIONS:
GET OUT OF THOSE SUITS RIGHT NOW...
OR I'M JUST GOING TO BURN THEM DOWN WITH YOU INSIDE THEM.

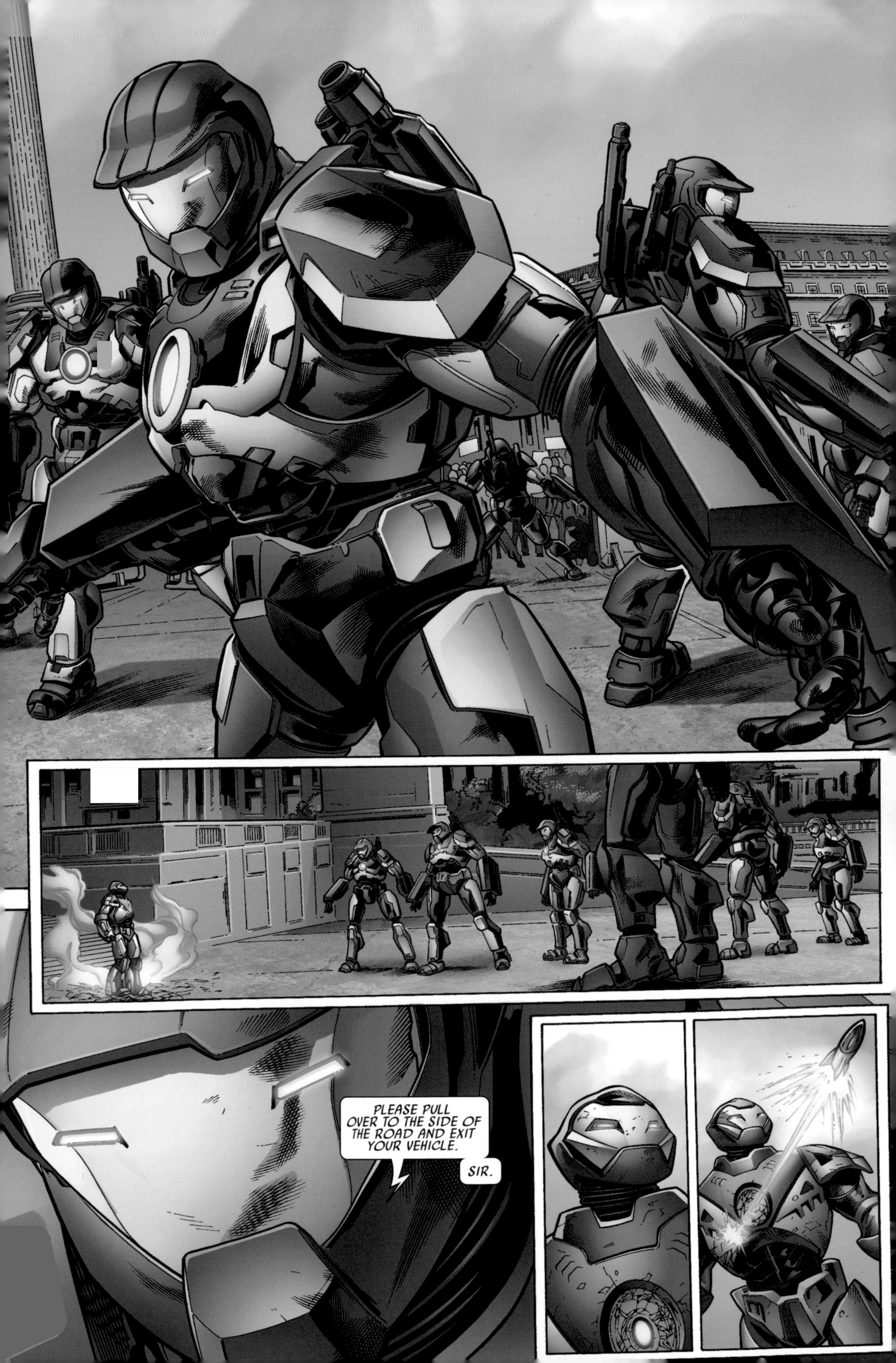
PLEASE PULL OVER TO THE SIDE OF THE ROAD AND EXIT YOUR VEHICLE.
SIR.

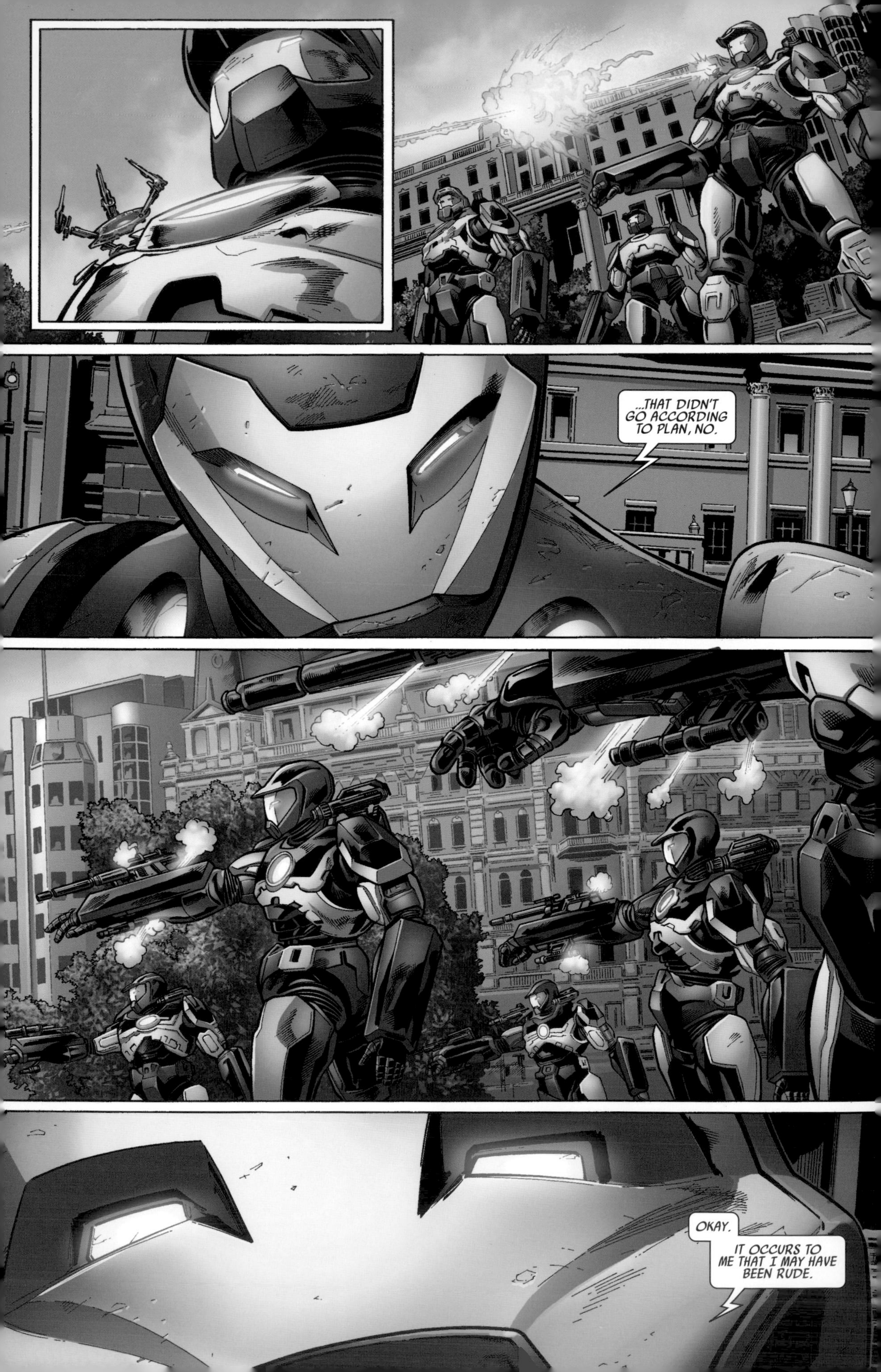
...THAT DIDN'T GO ACCORDING TO PLAN, NO.
OKAY.
IT OCCURS TO ME THAT I MAY HAVE BEEN RUDE.

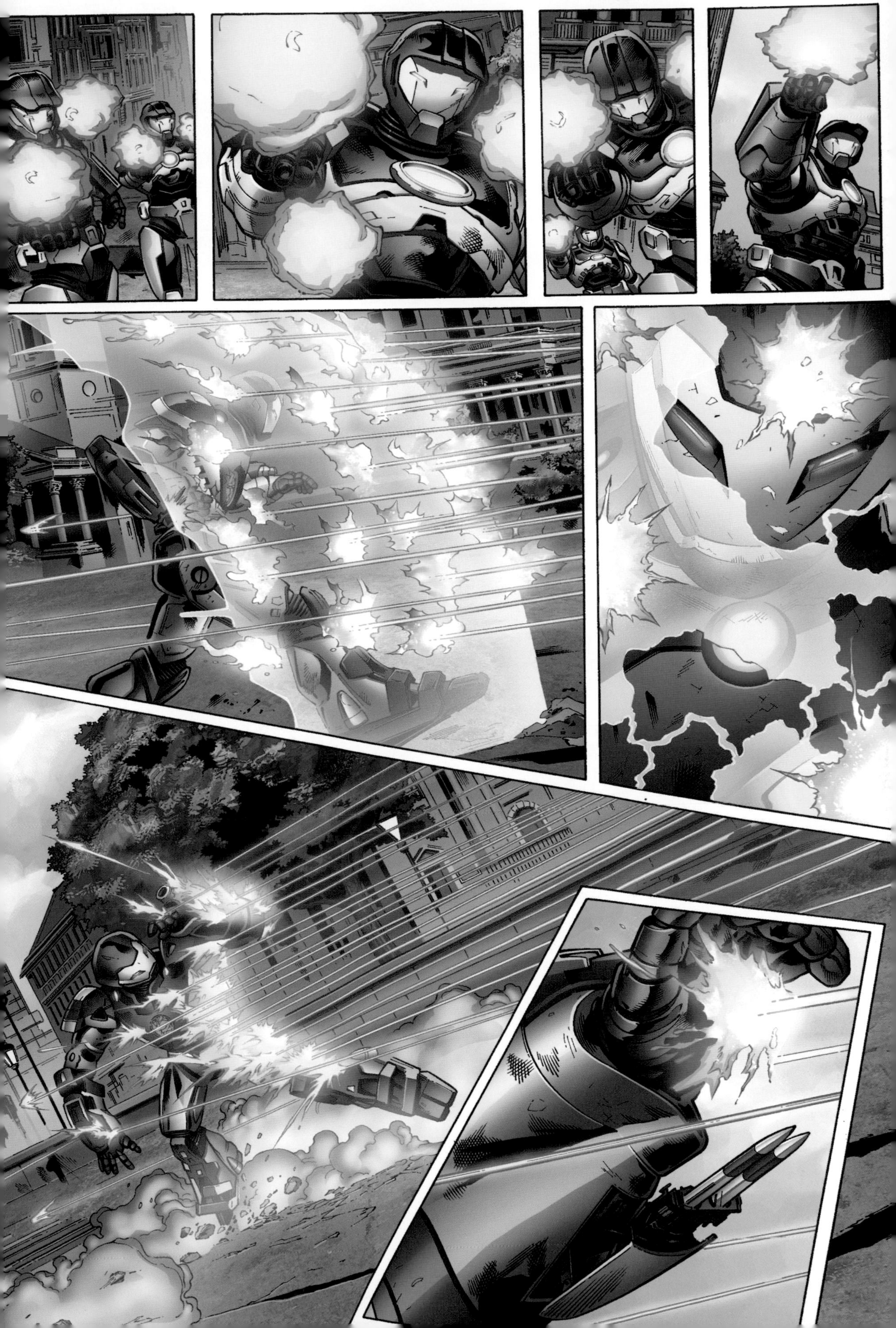

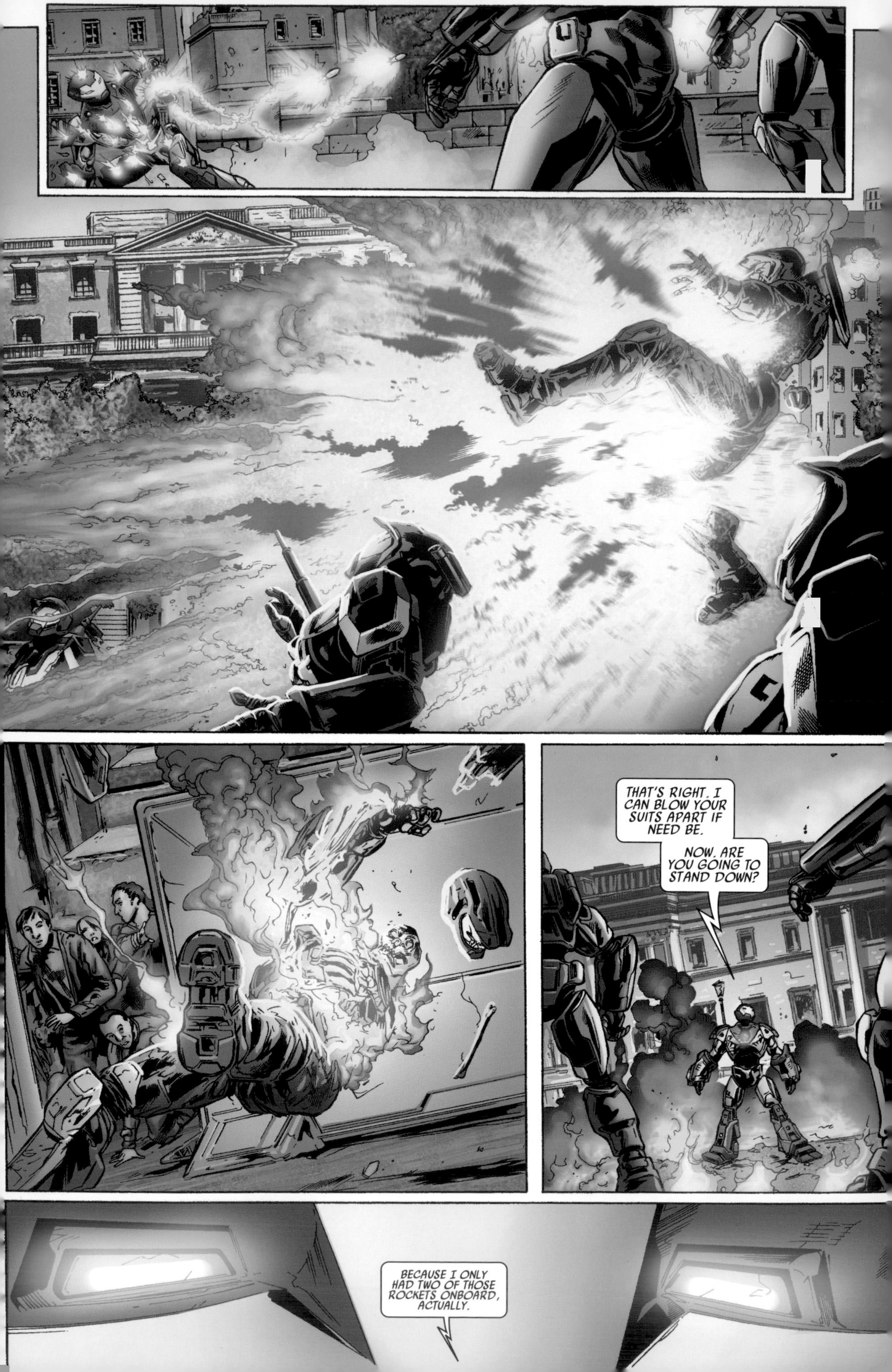
THAT'S RIGHT. I CAN BLOW YOUR SUITS APART IF NEED BE.
NOW. ARE YOU GOING TO STAND DOWN?
BECAUSE I ONLY HAD TWO OF THOSE ROCKETS ONBOARD, ACTUALLY.

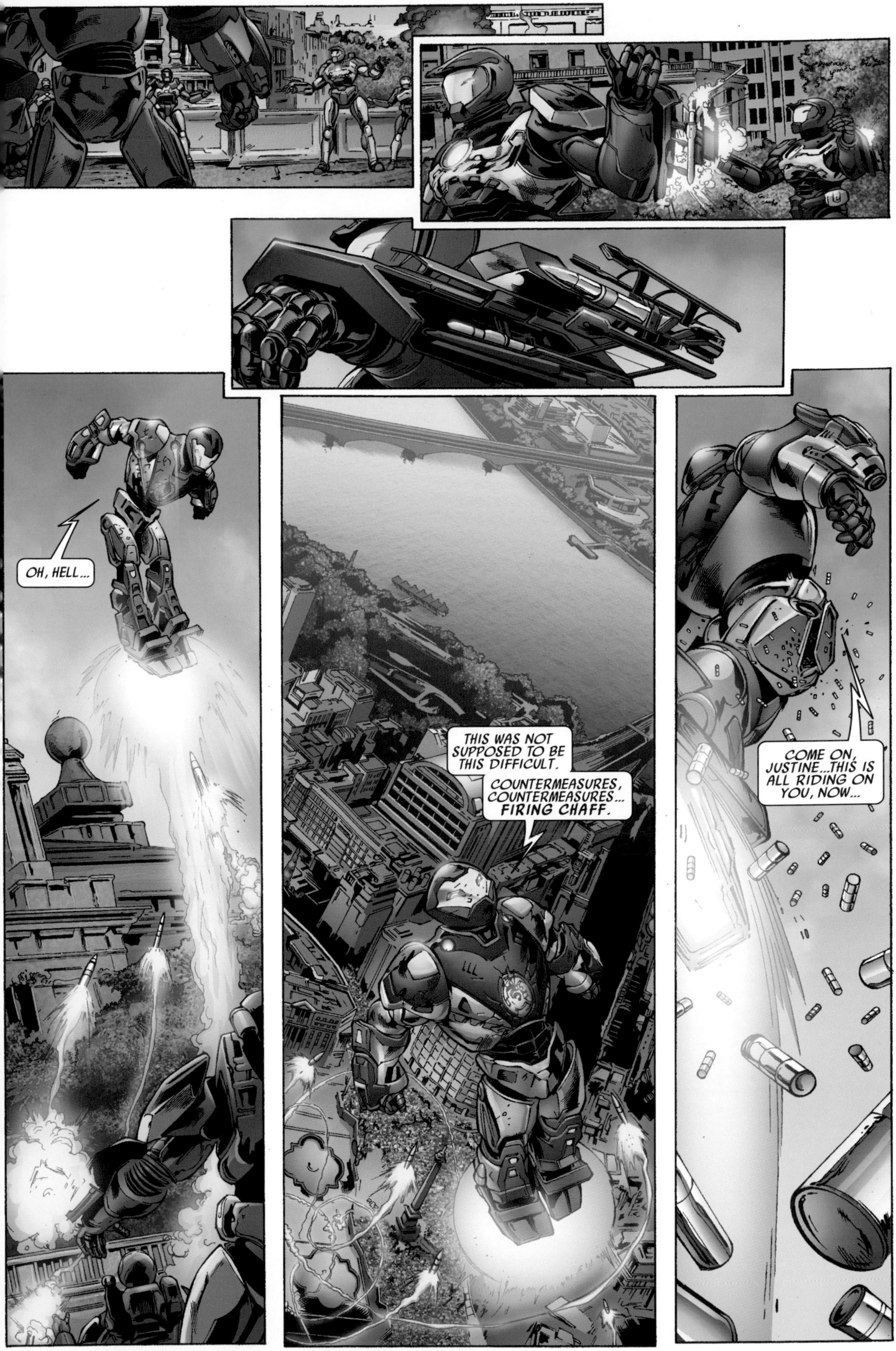
OH, HELL...
THIS WAS NOT SUPPOSED TO BE THIS DIFFICULT.
COUNTERMEASURES, COUNTERMEASURES... FIRING CHAFF.
COME ON, JUSTINE...THIS IS ALL RIDING ON YOU, NOW...

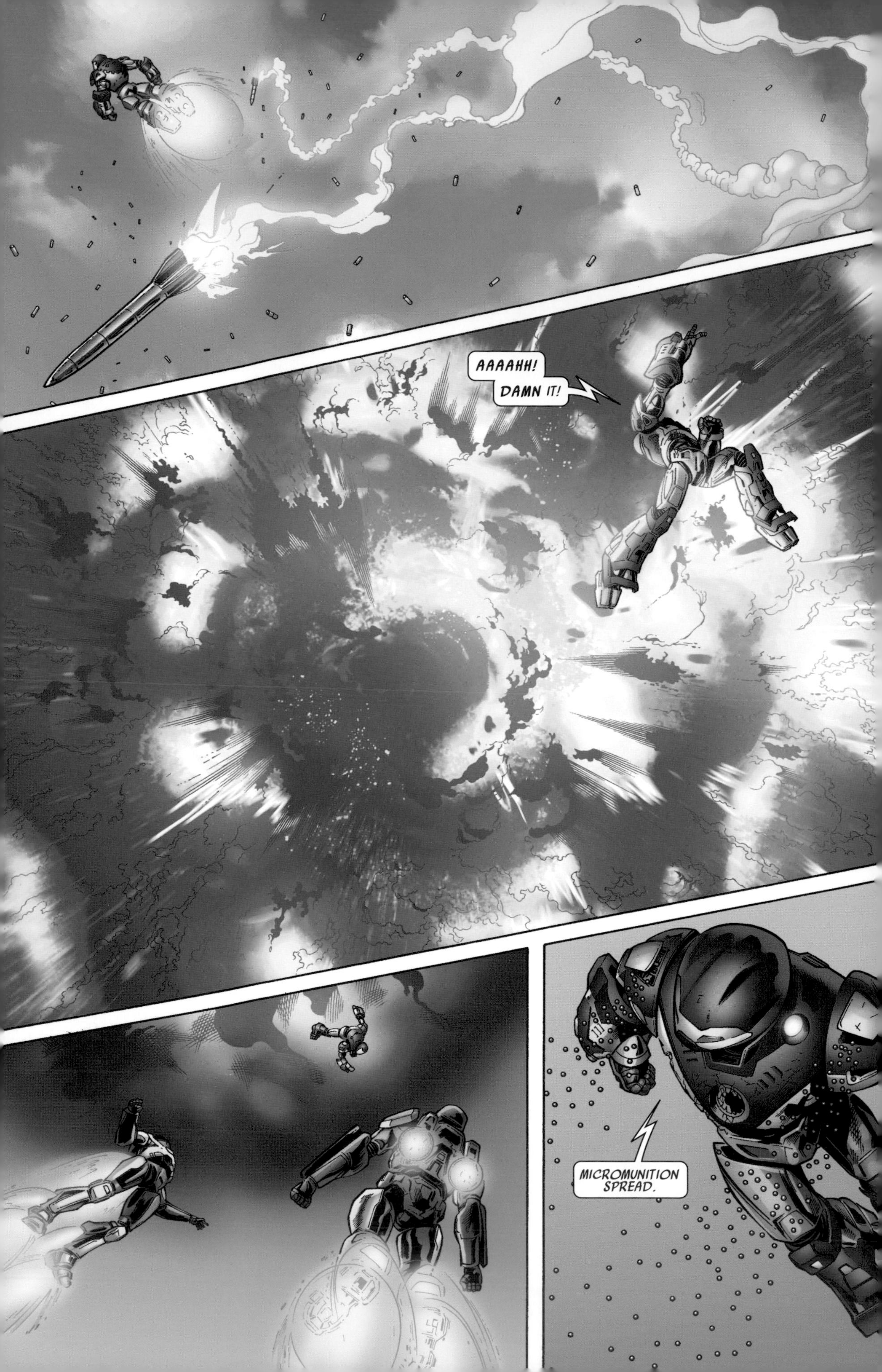
AAAAHH!
DAMN IT!
MICROMUNITION SPREAD.

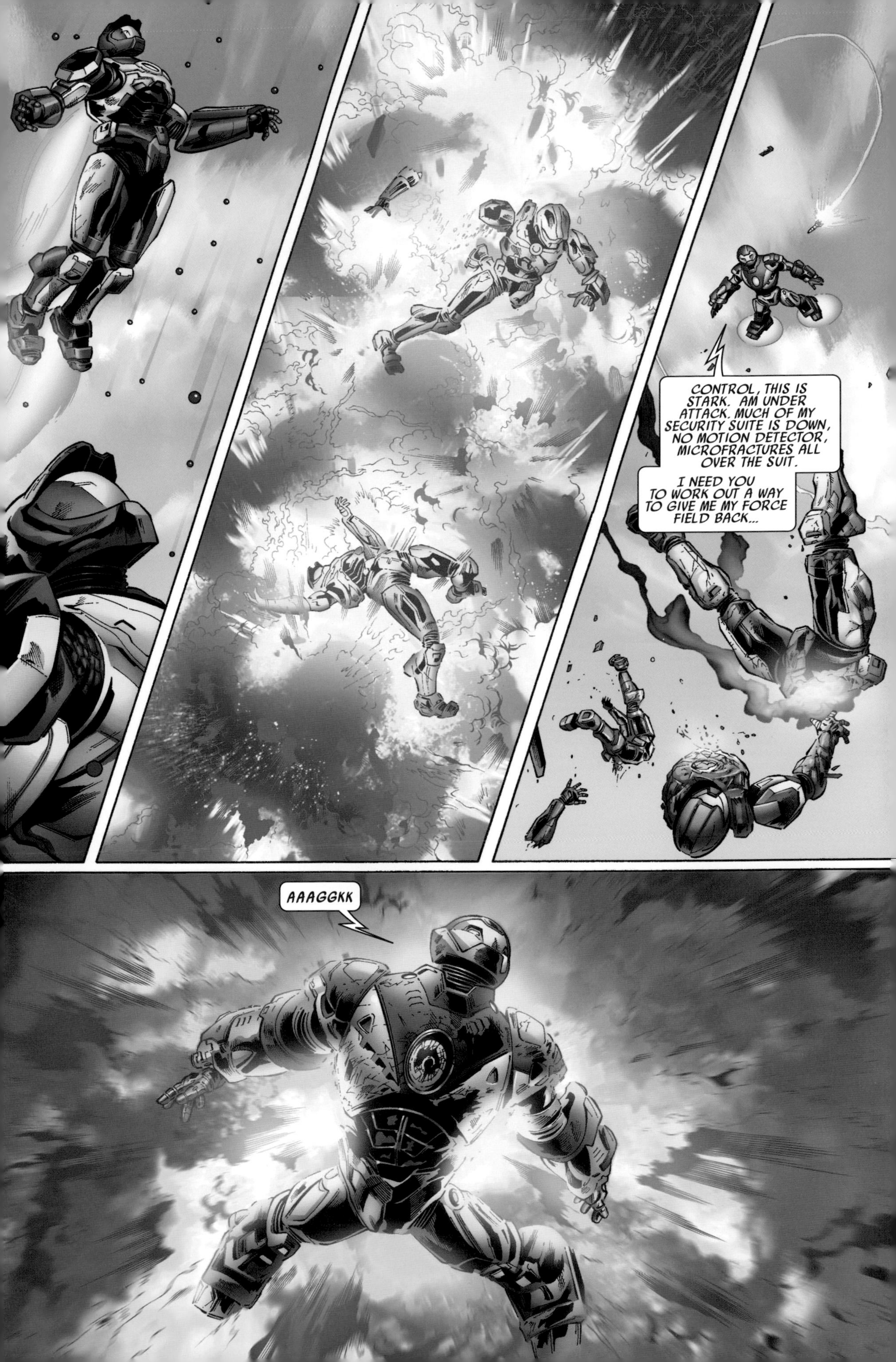
CONTROL, THIS IS STARK. AM UNDER ATTACK. MUCH OF MY SECURITY SUITE IS DOWN, NO MOTION DETECTOR, MICROFRACTURES ALL OVER THE SUIT.
I NEED YOU TO WORK OUT A WAY TO GIVE ME MY FORCE FIELD BACK...
AAAGGKK

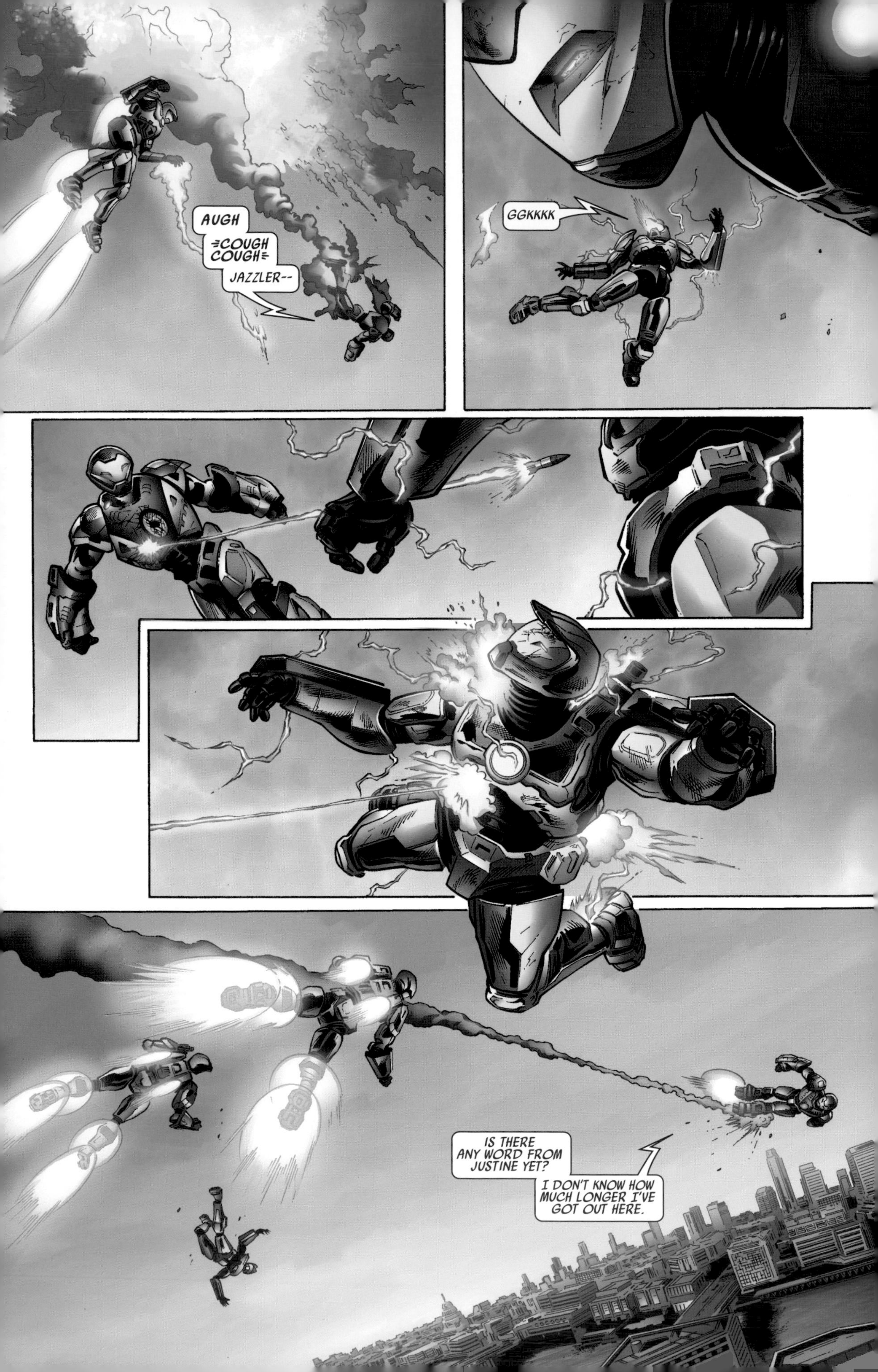
AUGH
COUGH COUGH
JAZZLER--
GGKKKK
IS THERE ANY WORD FROM JUSTINE YET?
I DON'T KNOW HOW MUCH LONGER I'VE GOT OUT HERE.

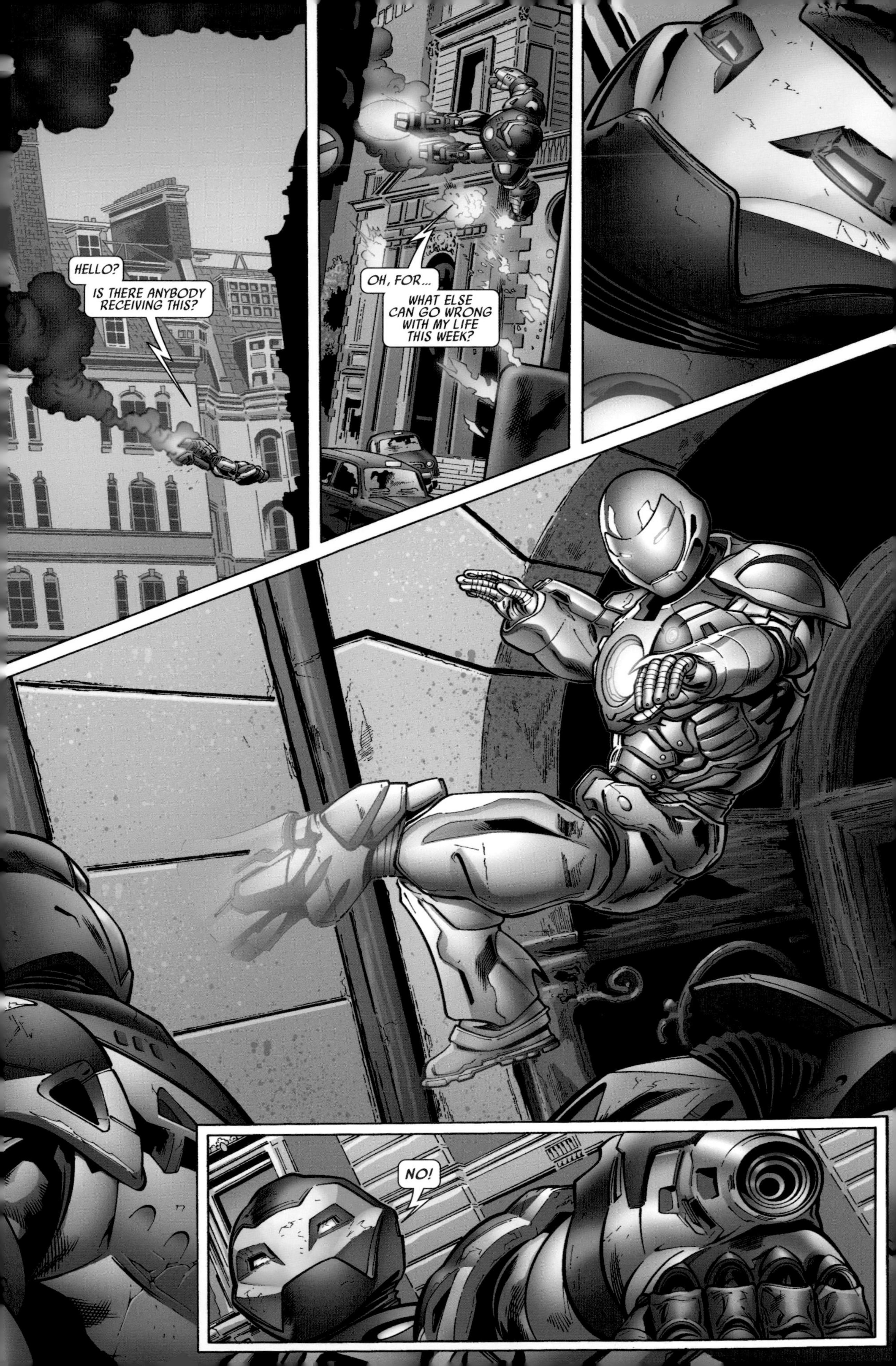
HELLO?
IS THERE ANYBODY RECEIVING THIS?
OH, FOR...
WHAT ELSE CAN GO WRONG WITH MY LIFE THIS WEEK?
NO!

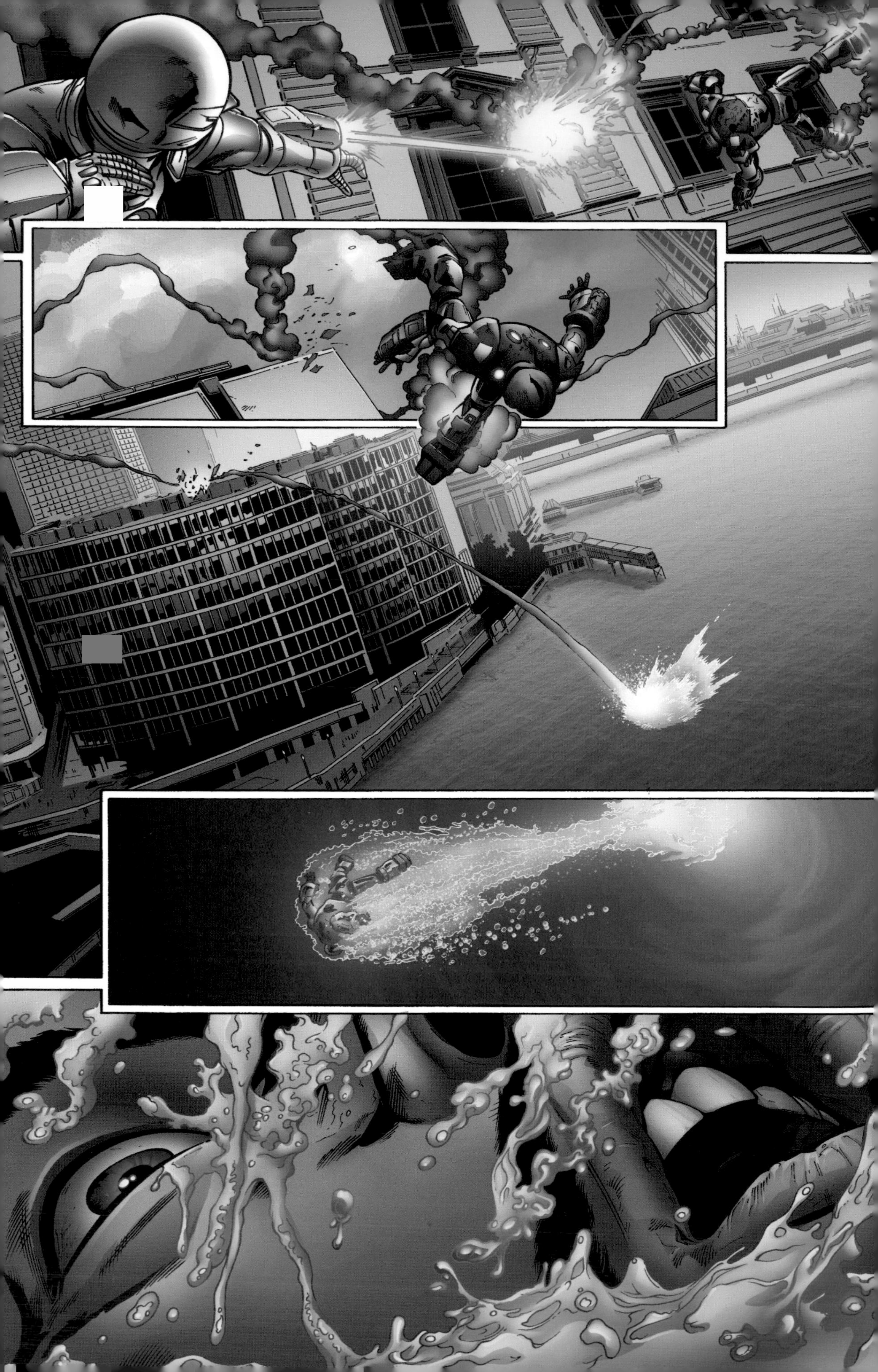

ULTIMATE ARMOUR WARS™

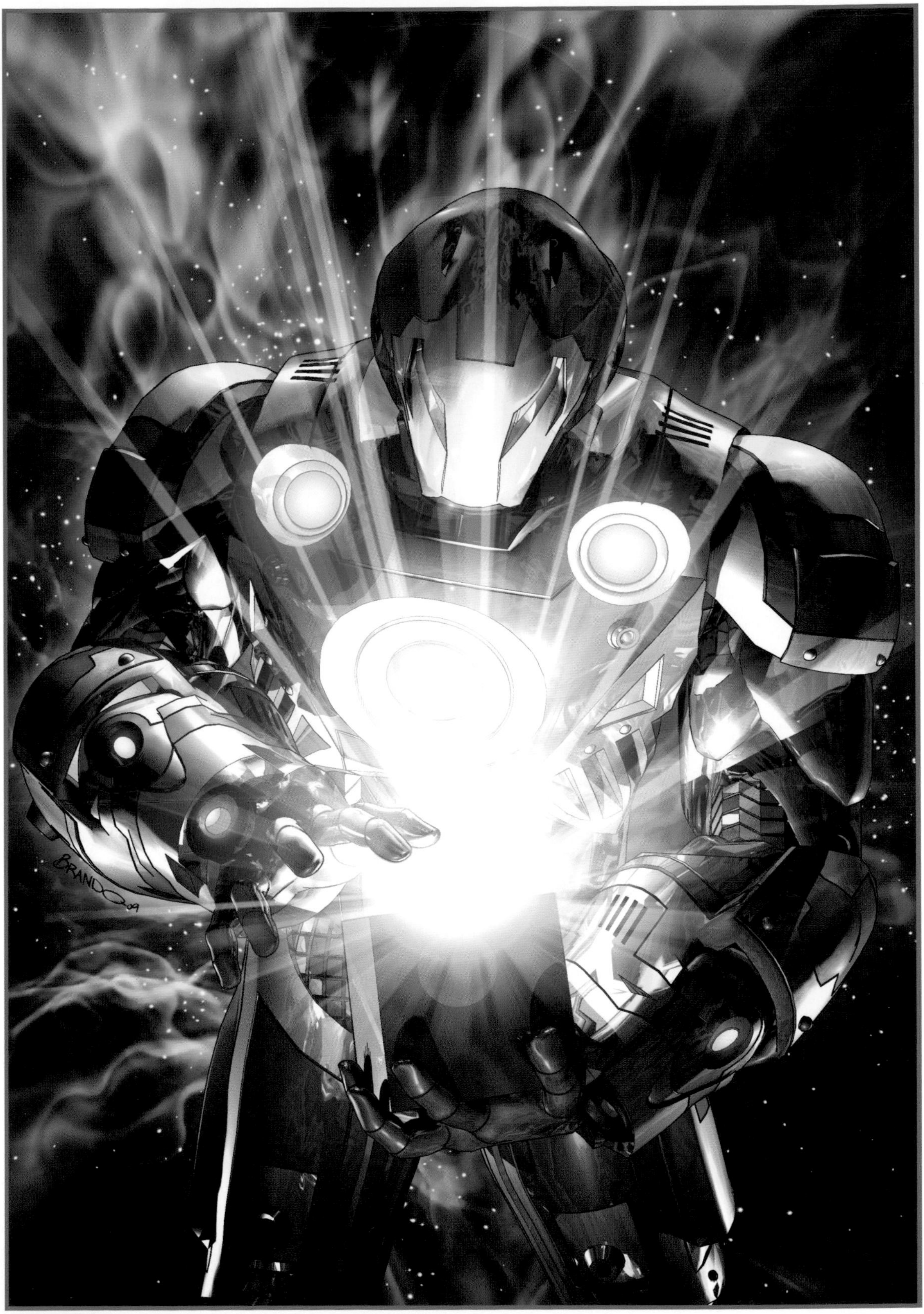
BRANDO 09

MARVEL®

ISSUE 004 COVER

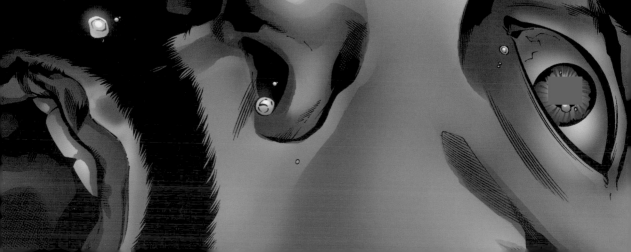

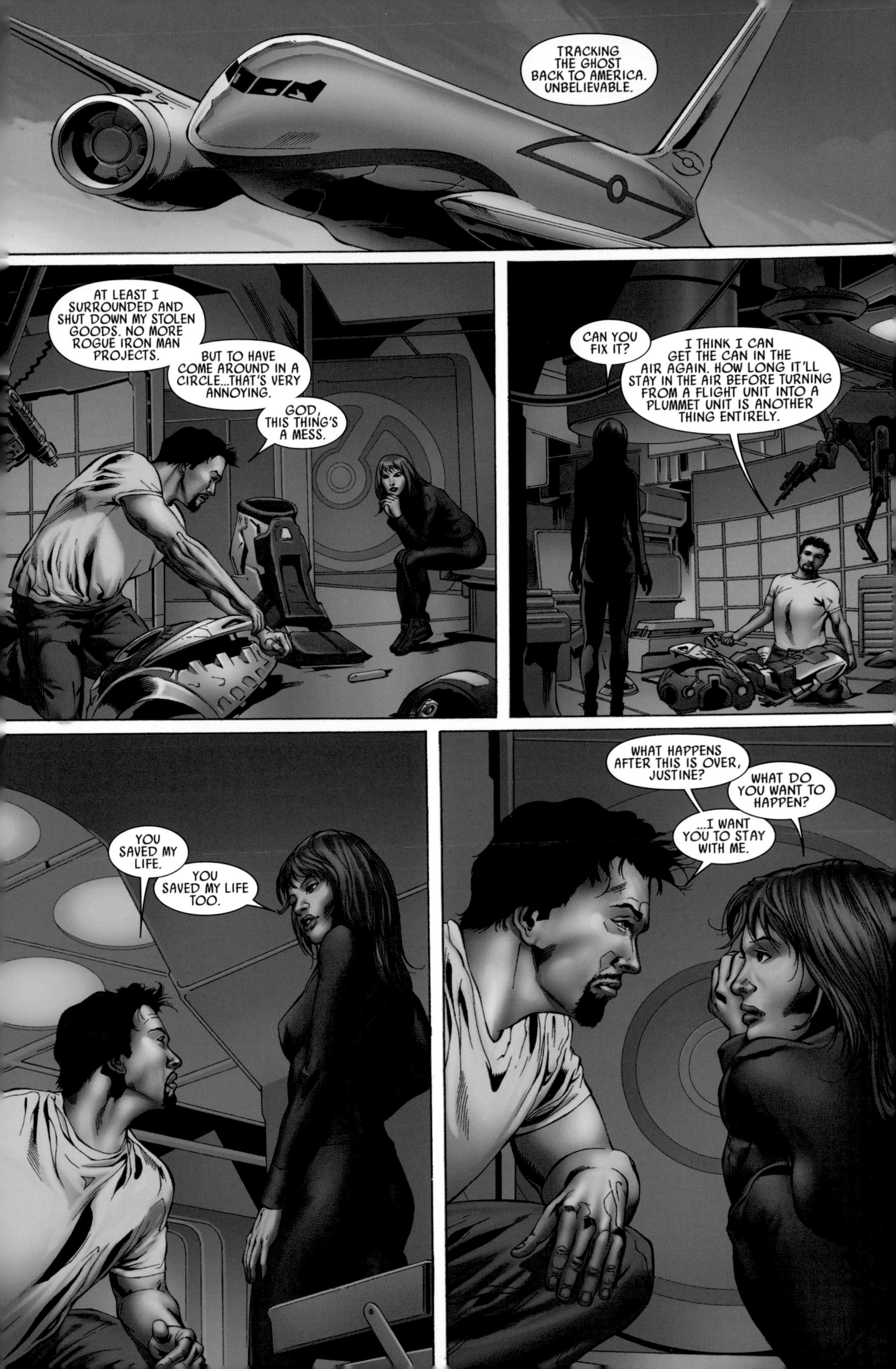
TRACKING THE GHOST BACK TO AMERICA. UNBELIEVABLE.
AT LEAST I SURROUNDED AND SHUT DOWN MY STOLEN GOODS. NO MORE ROGUE IRON MAN PROJECTS.
BUT TO HAVE COME AROUND IN A CIRCLE...THAT'S VERY ANNOYING.
GOD, THIS THING'S A MESS.
CAN YOU FIX IT?
I THINK I CAN GET THE CAN IN THE AIR AGAIN. HOW LONG IT'LL STAY IN THE AIR BEFORE TURNING FROM A FLIGHT UNIT INTO A PLUMMET UNIT IS ANOTHER THING ENTIRELY.
YOU SAVED MY LIFE.
YOU SAVED MY LIFE TOO.
WHAT HAPPENS AFTER THIS IS OVER, JUSTINE?
WHAT DO YOU WANT TO HAPPEN?
...I WANT YOU TO STAY WITH ME.

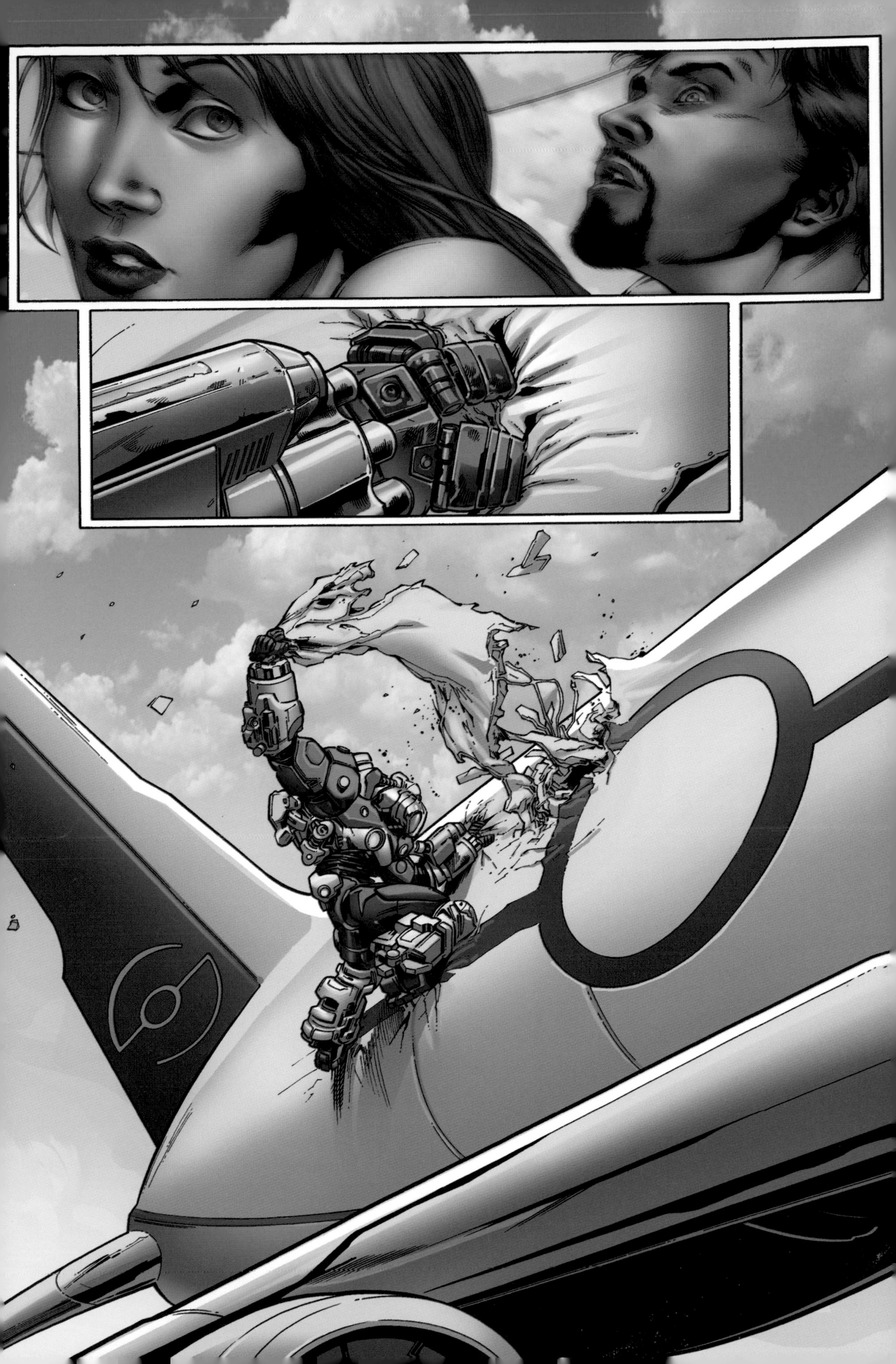

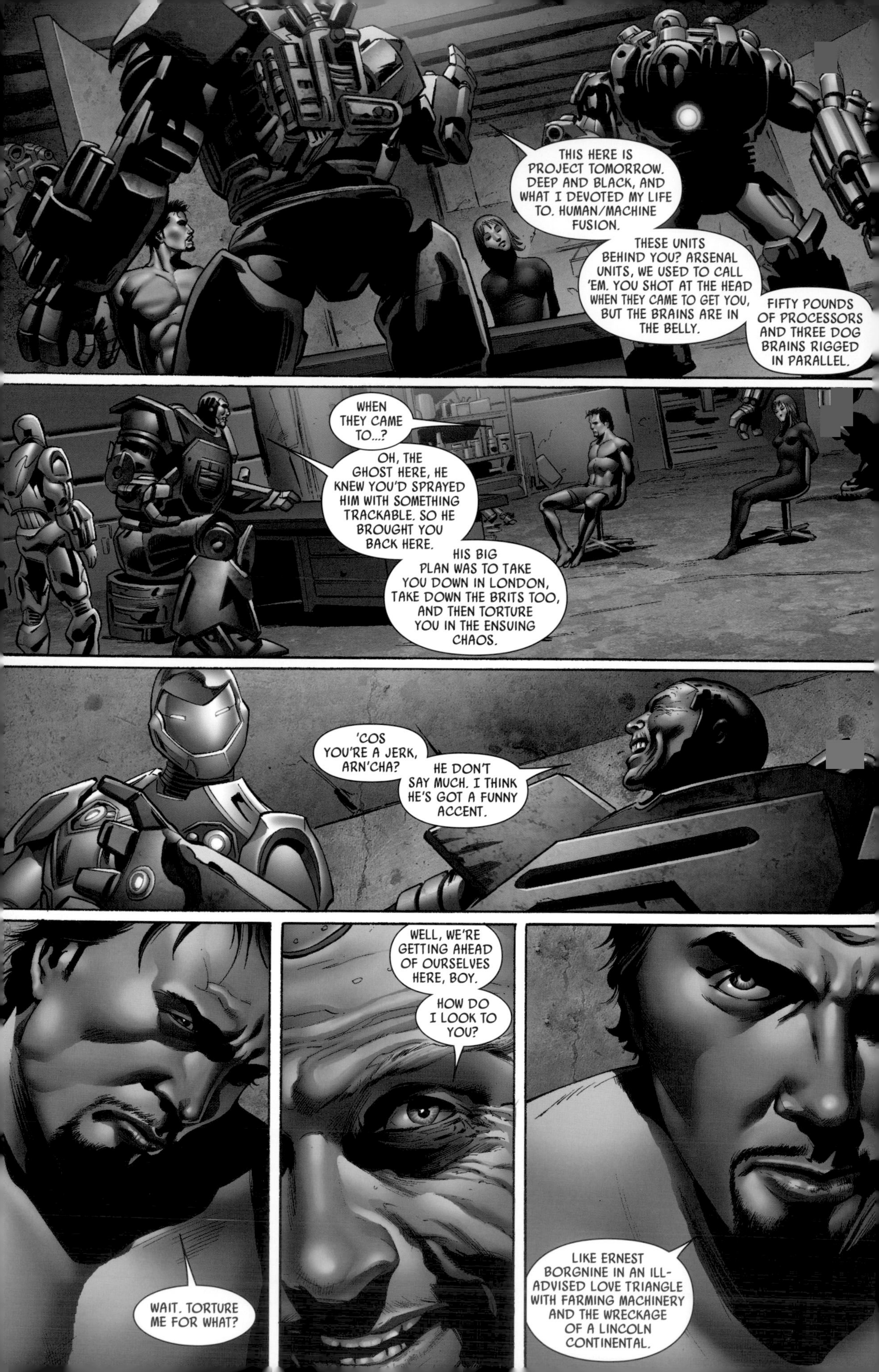
THIS HERE IS PROJECT TOMORROW. DEEP AND BLACK, AND WHAT I DEVOTED MY LIFE TO. HUMAN/MACHINE FUSION.
THESE UNITS BEHIND YOU? ARSENAL UNITS, WE USED TO CALL 'EM. YOU SHOT AT THE HEAD WHEN THEY CAME TO GET YOU, BUT THE BRAINS ARE IN THE BELLY.
FIFTY POUNDS OF PROCESSORS AND THREE DOG BRAINS RIGGED IN PARALLEL.
WHEN THEY CAME TO...?
OH, THE GHOST HERE, HE KNEW YOU'D SPRAYED HIM WITH SOMETHING TRACKABLE. SO HE BROUGHT YOU BACK HERE.
HIS BIG PLAN WAS TO TAKE YOU DOWN IN LONDON, TAKE DOWN THE BRITS TOO, AND THEN TORTURE YOU IN THE ENSUING CHAOS.
'COS YOU'RE A JERK, ARN'CHA?
HE DON'T SAY MUCH. I THINK HE'S GOT A FUNNY ACCENT.
WAIT. TORTURE ME FOR WHAT?
WELL, WE'RE GETTING AHEAD OF OURSELVES HERE, BOY.
HOW DO I LOOK TO YOU?
LIKE ERNEST BORGNINE IN AN ILL-ADVISED LOVE TRIANGLE WITH FARMING MACHINERY AND THE WRECKAGE OF A LINCOLN CONTINENTAL.

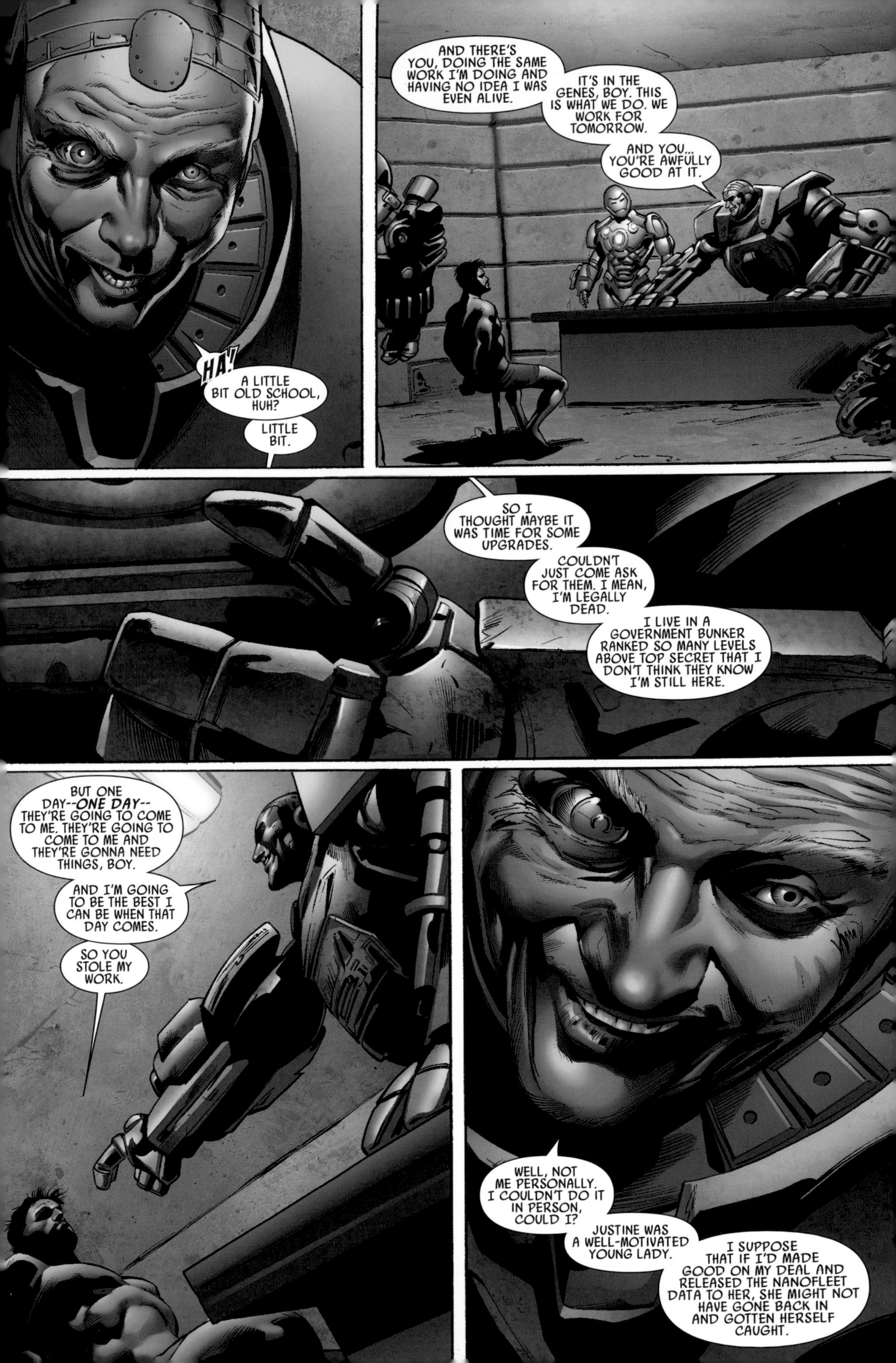
HA!
A LITTLE BIT OLD SCHOOL, HUH?
LITTLE BIT.
AND THERE'S YOU, DOING THE SAME WORK I'M DOING AND HAVING NO IDEA I WAS EVEN ALIVE.
IT'S IN THE GENES, BOY. THIS IS WHAT WE DO. WE WORK FOR TOMORROW.
AND YOU... YOU'RE AWFULLY GOOD AT IT.
SO I THOUGHT MAYBE IT WAS TIME FOR SOME UPGRADES.
COULDN'T JUST COME ASK FOR THEM. I MEAN, I'M LEGALLY DEAD.
I LIVE IN A GOVERNMENT BUNKER RANKED SO MANY LEVELS ABOVE TOP SECRET THAT I DON'T THINK THEY KNOW I'M STILL HERE.
BUT ONE DAY--ONE DAY--THEY'RE GOING TO COME TO ME. THEY'RE GOING TO COME TO ME AND THEY'RE GONNA NEED THINGS, BOY.
AND I'M GOING TO BE THE BEST I CAN BE WHEN THAT DAY COMES.
SO YOU STOLE MY WORK.
WELL, NOT ME PERSONALLY. I COULDN'T DO IT IN PERSON, COULD I?
JUSTINE WAS A WELL-MOTIVATED YOUNG LADY.
I SUPPOSE THAT IF I'D MADE GOOD ON MY DEAL AND RELEASED THE NANOFLEET DATA TO HER, SHE MIGHT NOT HAVE GONE BACK IN AND GOTTEN HERSELF CAUGHT.

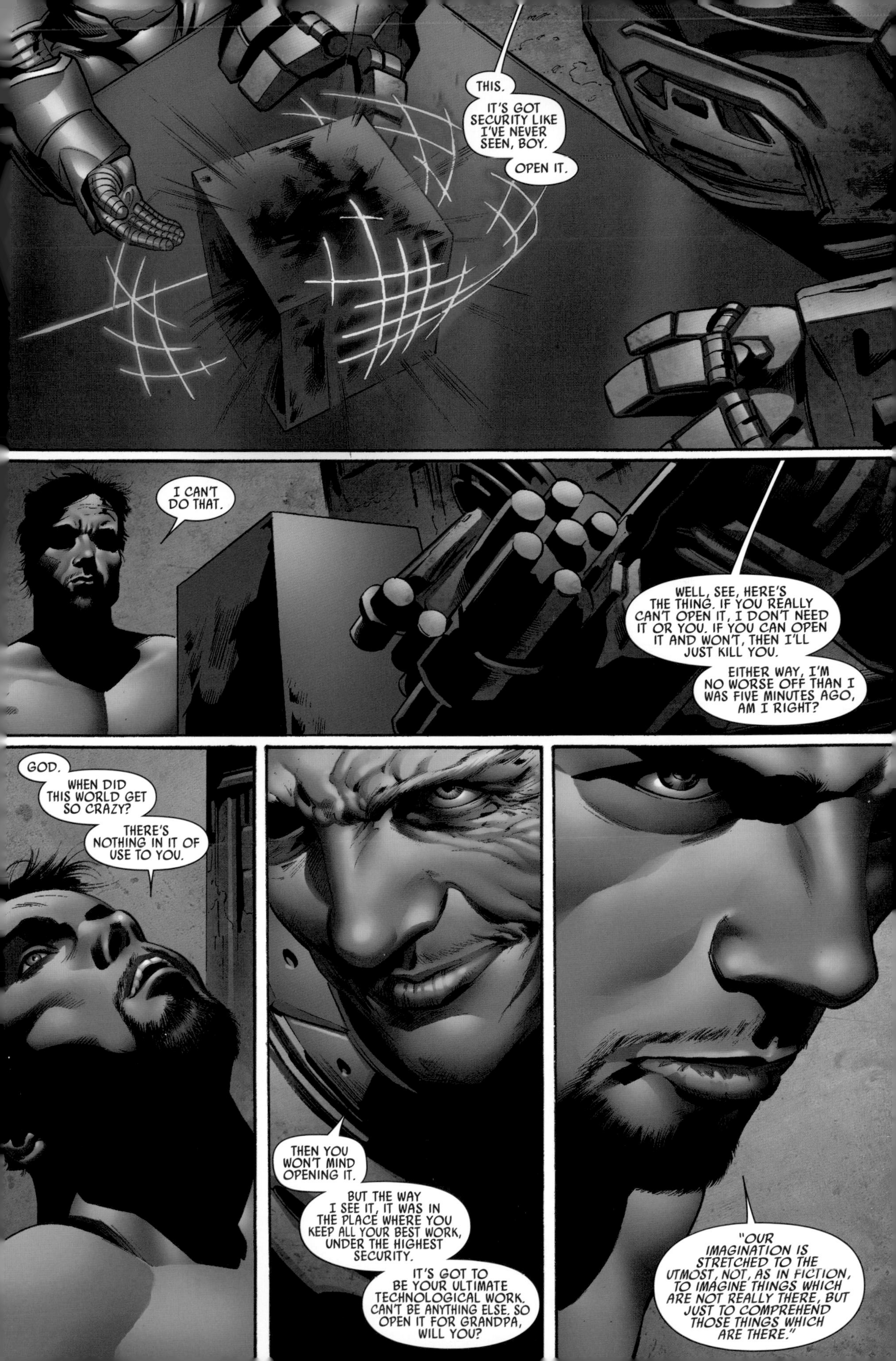
THIS.
IT'S GOT SECURITY LIKE I'VE NEVER SEEN, BOY.
OPEN IT.
I CAN'T DO THAT.
WELL, SEE, HERE'S THE THING. IF YOU REALLY CAN'T OPEN IT, I DON'T NEED IT OR YOU. IF YOU CAN OPEN IT AND WON'T, THEN I'LL JUST KILL YOU.
EITHER WAY, I'M NO WORSE OFF THAN I WAS FIVE MINUTES AGO, AM I RIGHT?
GOD.
WHEN DID THIS WORLD GET SO CRAZY?
THERE'S NOTHING IN IT OF USE TO YOU.
THEN YOU WON'T MIND OPENING IT.
BUT THE WAY I SEE IT, IT WAS IN THE PLACE WHERE YOU KEEP ALL YOUR BEST WORK, UNDER THE HIGHEST SECURITY.
IT'S GOT TO BE YOUR ULTIMATE TECHNOLOGICAL WORK. CAN'T BE ANYTHING ELSE. SO OPEN IT FOR GRANDPA, WILL YOU?
"OUR IMAGINATION IS STRETCHED TO THE UTMOST, NOT, AS IN FICTION, TO IMAGINE THINGS WHICH ARE NOT REALLY THERE, BUT JUST TO COMPREHEND THOSE THINGS WHICH ARE THERE."

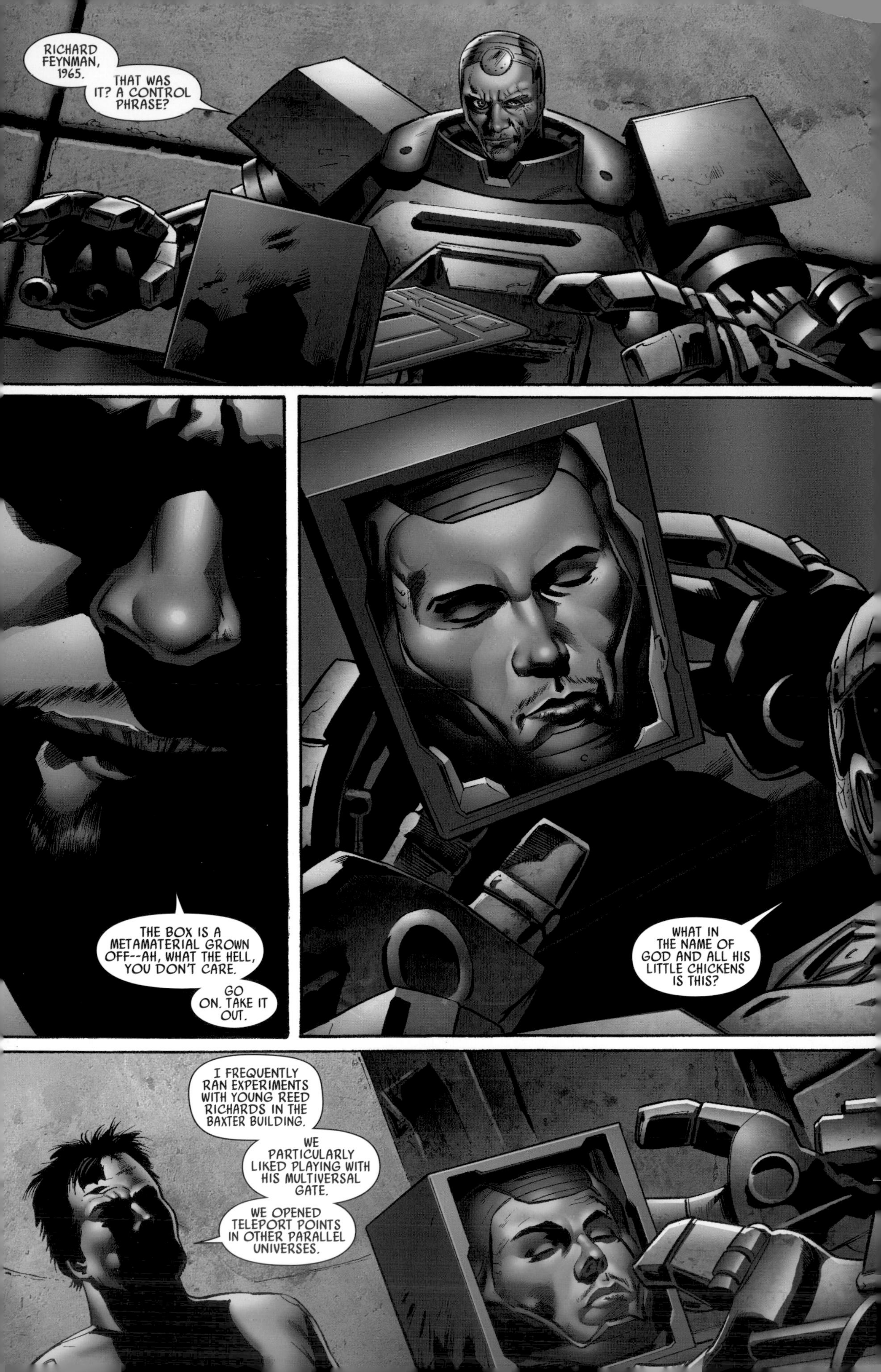

RICHARD FEYNMAN, 1965.
THAT WAS IT? A CONTROL PHRASE?
THE BOX IS A METAMATERIAL GROWN OFF--AH, WHAT THE HELL, YOU DON'T CARE.
GO ON. TAKE IT OUT.
WHAT IN THE NAME OF GOD AND ALL HIS LITTLE CHICKENS IS THIS?
I FREQUENTLY RAN EXPERIMENTS WITH YOUNG REED RICHARDS IN THE BAXTER BUILDING.
WE PARTICULARLY LIKED PLAYING WITH HIS MULTIVERSAL GATE.
WE OPENED TELEPORT POINTS IN OTHER PARALLEL UNIVERSES.

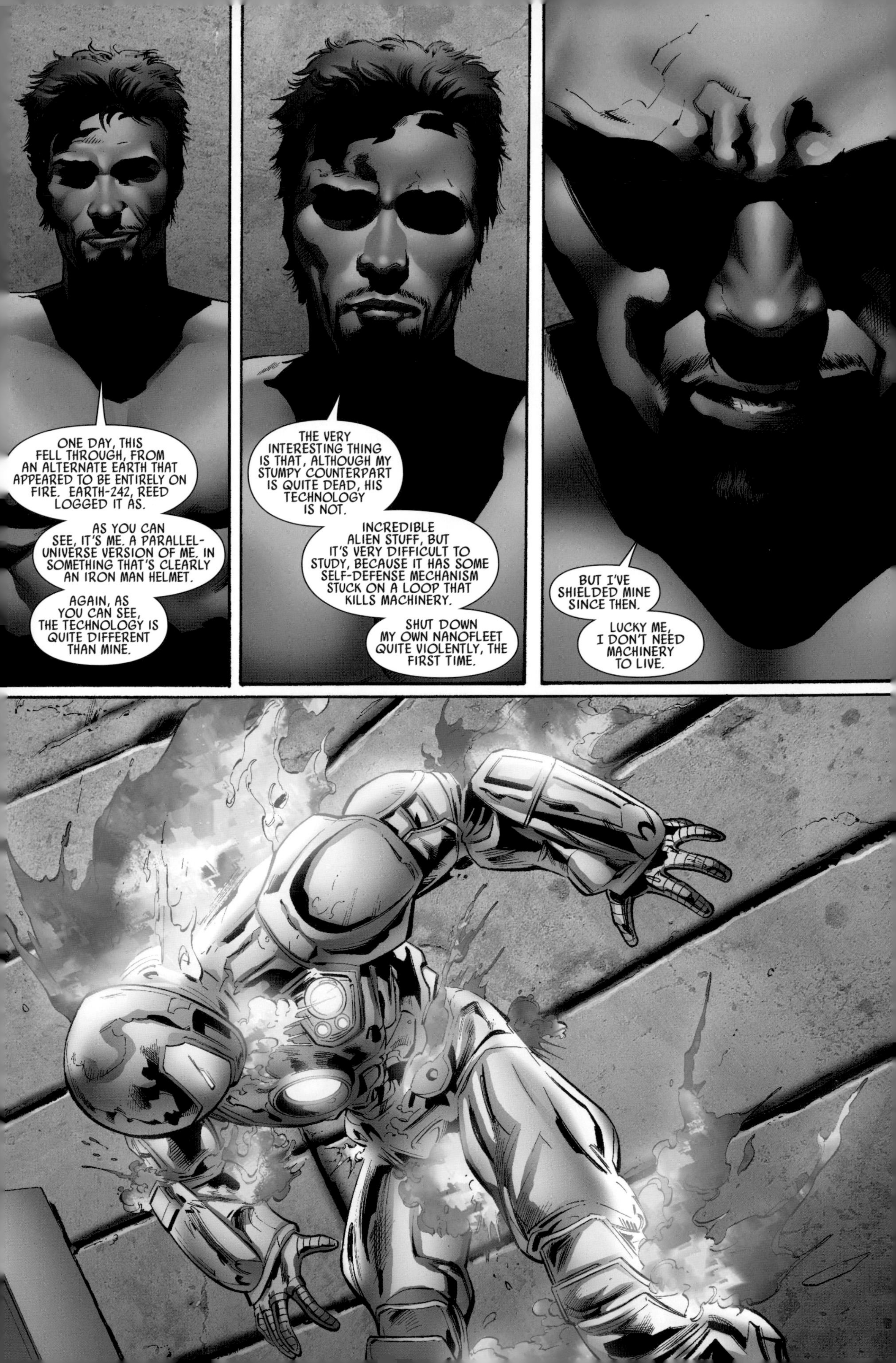
ONE DAY, THIS FELL THROUGH, FROM AN ALTERNATE EARTH THAT APPEARED TO BE ENTIRELY ON FIRE. EARTH-242, REED LOGGED IT AS.
AS YOU CAN SEE, IT'S ME. A PARALLEL-UNIVERSE VERSION OF ME. IN SOMETHING THAT'S CLEARLY AN IRON MAN HELMET.
AGAIN, AS YOU CAN SEE, THE TECHNOLOGY IS QUITE DIFFERENT THAN MINE.
THE VERY INTERESTING THING IS THAT, ALTHOUGH MY STUMPY COUNTERPART IS QUITE DEAD, HIS TECHNOLOGY IS NOT.
INCREDIBLE ALIEN STUFF, BUT IT'S VERY DIFFICULT TO STUDY, BECAUSE IT HAS SOME SELF-DEFENSE MECHANISM STUCK ON A LOOP THAT KILLS MACHINERY.
SHUT DOWN MY OWN NANOFLEET QUITE VIOLENTLY, THE FIRST TIME.
BUT I'VE SHIELDED MINE SINCE THEN.
LUCKY ME, I DON'T NEED MACHINERY TO LIVE.

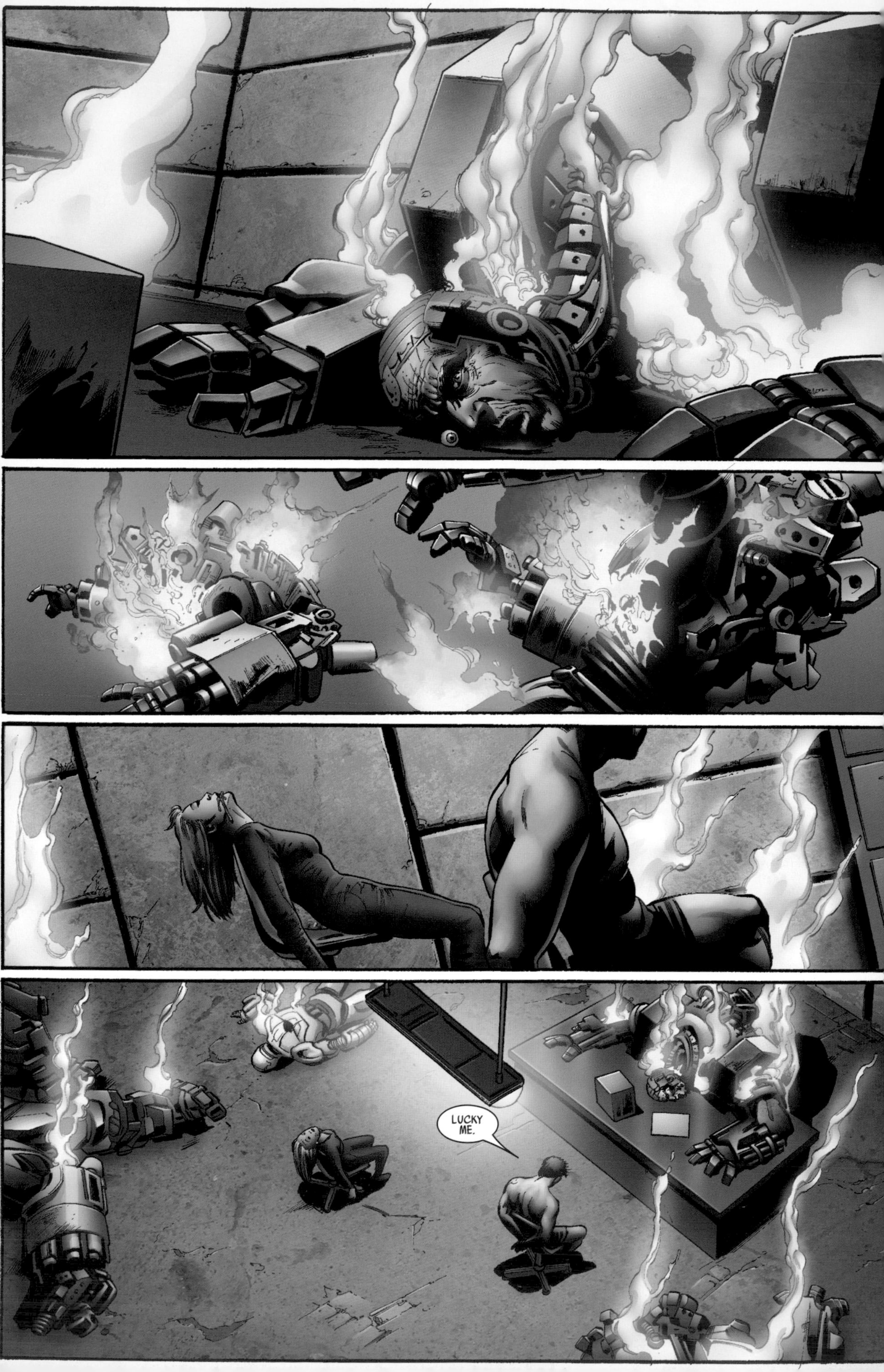
LUCKY ME.

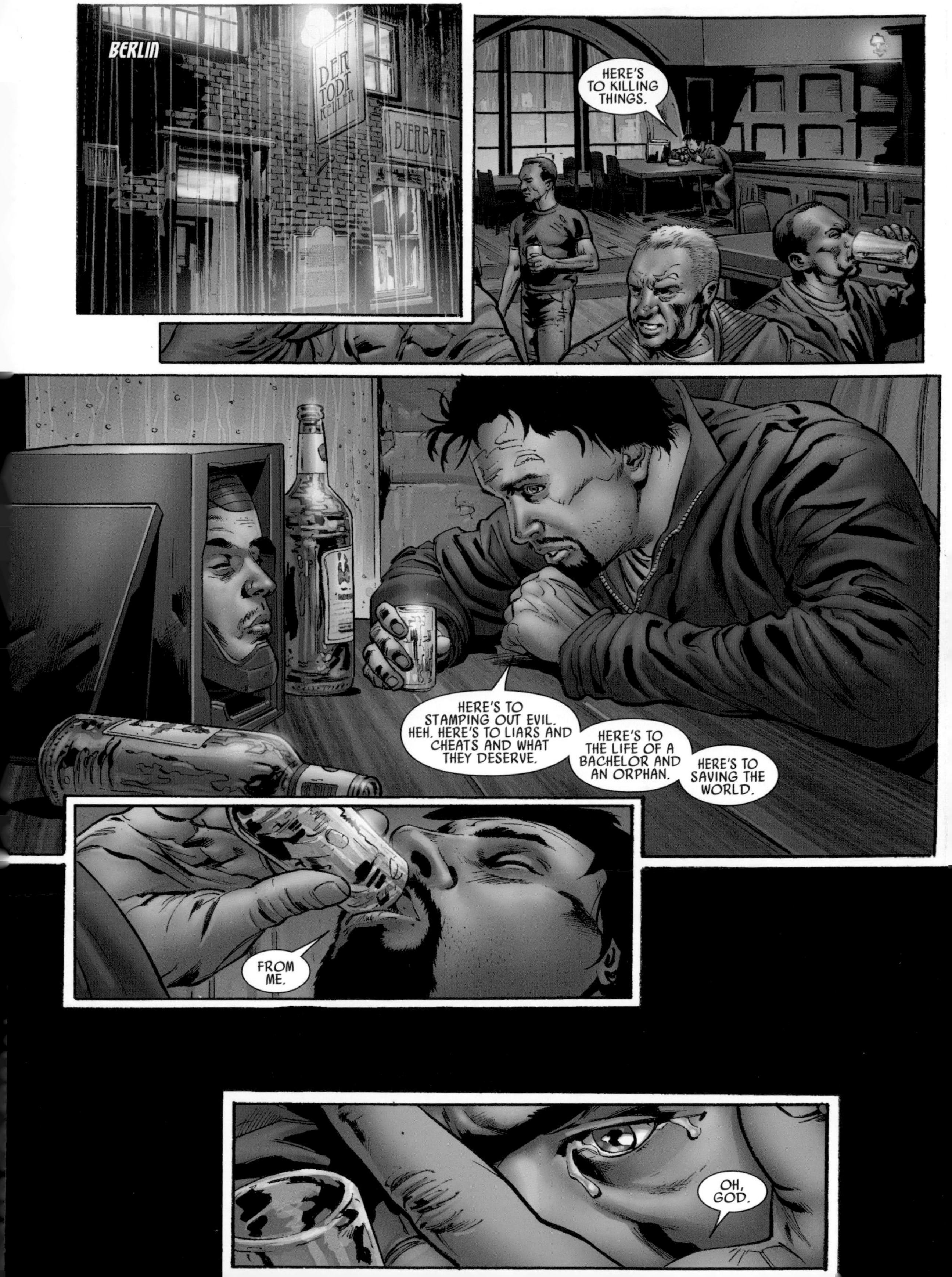
BERLIN
DER TODT KELLER
BIERBAR
HERE'S TO KILLING THINGS.
HERE'S TO STAMPING OUT EVIL. HEH. HERE'S TO LIARS AND CHEATS AND WHAT THEY DESERVE.
HERE'S TO THE LIFE OF A BACHELOR AND AN ORPHAN.
HERE'S TO SAVING THE WORLD.
FROM ME.
OH, GOD.